A MATTER OF
Life
and
Breath

A MATTER OF

Life
and
Breath

My 7 Step Guide to
Overcoming Near Death From
Long CoVid and Pulmonary Fibrosis

LEE FOGLE

This book is dedicated to my children,
Nick, Bryan, and Katie.

"Living a long, healthy life is like walking across a minefield; if you see footprints to the other side, walk in them"

CONTENTS

FOREWORD

I first met Lee Fogle in late 2021, on the other side of the computer screen through a telehealth visit. His sentences were short and breathy, interrupted by coughing fits and periods of rest, in an attempt to catch his breath. He appeared thin, chronically ill, with a nasal cannula in his nose, delivering continuous oxygen. As I asked him questions about his current illness, I typed out the words, unknown respiratory illness, pneumonia, pulmonary emboli, pulmonary fibrosis, and long haul COVID. I also typed out the words athlete, training, triathlon. Surely the man I was seeing on the other side of the screen never partook in athletics. Prior to our meeting, his life was severely changed in less than a year. He had been to specialists, had multiple CT scans, and was left with answers that offered no hope. He was left searching, only to look forward to an unknown future of fighting for air.

How was I going to help this man? I am no expert in my field. How did he find me and what makes him think I can help him? "Just listen to him," I coached myself. Maybe this is a dying request, to simply be heard, to know that he exhausted all efforts to redeem his health. Long haul COVID was a newly emerging medical condition, with little being published about how to truly help these patients.

Despite the complexity of his illness, Lee showed up to his visits with questions and ideas he had already researched. We discussed off label medications, alternative treatments, newly emerging protocols. He also showed up to each appointment with goals, short and long term goals. This man had future goals of running, biking, and swimming again. This man, who couldn't even walk down his hallway without becoming short of breath, had future goals? I have to admit, there were days I looked into that computer screen and held back tears. I wanted him to succeed, to beat his current diagnosis, to pursue these goals, but his future looked grim.

I desperately wanted to refer him to pulmonology, as I did not feel equipped with the knowledge to provide the level of care this patient required. I even tried to refer him at one point, but Lee just kept showing up to appointments, and I eventually realized, he was not going to give up. Not only did Lee show up for himself, he started showing up for others, volunteering with hospice and support groups for others suffering from pulmonary fibrosis.

Our appointments became brainstorming sessions of new ideas, medications, testing options. CT scans started showing improvement, vitals started to improve, Lee started to gain weight, he was biking and walking with oxygen. I even remember one visit where he forgot to turn his oxygen on and made it through the entire appointment without knowing.

Persevere, nevertheless, in spite of, against all odds.... These are all words I could use to describe Lee as he navigated through his difficult diagnoses. He refused to sit idle, he chose to take control of his health and seek answers. While Lee is not cured of his current illness, I can't even say that he has learned to live with it. I would say that Lee Fogle is thriving, inspiring others along the way, despite his circumstances. I'm not sure I have ever learned so much from a patient, but I do know that I am proud to know Lee and be part of his journey.

Ashley Dunmire APRN, FNP-C

INTRODUCTION

The 7 Step process of recovery that follows is a logical process that is best followed in the specific order. Some of these 7 steps you may already be excellent at, but taking the time to build them into your life from the ground up will ensure your successful recovery of your lung health and overall physical health.

1. First, without a **vision** you're just going through the motions. You must have a **vision of success**; it is fundamental to everything that follows.
2. But the vision is not magic by itself. You must also have a plan that acknowledges where you are and how to achieve your vision. That plan naturally includes **goals and methods** to achieve them and continually measuring your progress.
3. Once that's completed you're ready to activate the plan. Activation starts inside you, a balanced, composed, noise free inner peace to operate from. **Meditation** establishes that calm center.
4. Following that you must evaluate your current **breathing** mechanics, and then follow a proven plan to improve how you breathe while strengthening your lungs and diaphragm with daily breathing exercises. Proper improved oxygenation of the whole body is the result.

5. With this solid base of vision, composure and proper breathing you're ready to **exercise** with purpose. It will be hard, but start where you are and gradually increase, the improvement of your health will follow.

6. Without proper rest you cannot achieve a level of health and vigor necessary to recover, so proper **sleep** is crucial. It will become the most nourishing time of your day.

7. Lastly, in spite of all the good you are doing, you can still commit "nutritional suicide" unless you have excellent **nutrition**. Much of what you and most folks in America eat are the direct causes of age-related diseases and contribute to the leading causes of death. It is highly likely that your diet must change significantly to support your recovery.

The success I've experienced in life has been the result of following the advice of people who've already done what I was attempting. I learned not to overthink it, but just to have the discipline to follow what's already been proven to work. The 7 Steps in this book have taken me from near death with end stage pulmonary fibrosis and less than 30% lung function to a return to a healthy and active life with twice the lung function I had previously. I am fully living again.

NOTE: I receive no compensation, commission, or royalties for any of the products mentioned in this book. I mention particular brand names simply because I've tried several and found that these brand names worked best for me.

DISCLAIMER This book is for general informational purposes only and does not constitute the practice of medicine, nursing, or other professional health care services, including the giving of medical advice, and no doctor/patient relationship is formed. The use of information from this book, podcast or materials linked from this book is at the user's own risk. The content of this book is not intended to be a substitute for professional medical advice, diagnosis, or treatment. Users should not disregard or delay in obtaining medical advice for any medical condition they may have and should seek the assistance of their health care professionals for any such conditions.

Chapter 1

Before you is a fork in the road as you begin this book. You have a decision to make. You can choose to do everything you can to recover your health and enjoy your life, or you can choose to be bitter and feel miserable about your circumstances, and hopeless about your life. I have met many people in the latter category in my journey through lung disease. I have also met some folks who have outlived the 3 to 5 year life expectancy of advanced pulmonary fibrosis, some by more than 10 years, and they're still going strong. They are actively living with great attitudes and health, enjoying their family and friends and fully participating in and enjoying life.

As you read this book, I want to set your expectations for a new quality of life through the principles I've used to completely transform my health in just over 14 months.

What you'll learn, and become, if you apply the principles in this book:

1. **You will take authority over your health and** set your mind on a vision of recovery and a full, active life.

2. **You will have a written vision for your life,** with a set of goals that you will use to actively manage and measure your progress.

3. You will learn a simple daily meditation that will promote a healing mindset. **You will be like a rock, unshaken by fear or worry.**

4. You will fully engage and retrain your breathing muscles, and consequently **maximize your lung function and cardiovascular health, resulting in better oxygenation of your brain and body.**

5. You will create and actively follow an exercise program tailored for your current health situation, that will become increasingly strenuous. **This will result in your improved cardiovascular fitness, better overall oxygenation, muscle fitness, prevention of falls and injuries to bones and joints, lower blood pressure, greater stamina, and greater satisfaction with your life.**

6. You will create your own formula for **maximizing the healthy benefits of sleep, that will improve your mental clarity and overall health through sleeping restfully each night.**

7. You will create a nutritional diet that will **dramatically lower your risk of disease, heart attack, high blood pressure, and diabetes, significantly improving your lung function.**

8. You will assume an **active role in your health recovery,** and you will work collaboratively with your physician to take authority over the improvement of your health.

9. You **will become more fun for others to be around, your social relationships will improve, and you will find purpose in your life,** whether

it's through your hobbies, new creative outlets, or volunteering in your community to help others.

10. **Others will be amazed by your optimistic attitude toward life, and the life wisdom that you have to pass along to the next generation**.

Every day on earth about 200,000 people die. Most did not see it coming. None of us are promised anything more than today, but we can live as if it is our last day, and enjoy this life, making an impact on the world around us. I cannot promise you that if you follow the methods that I have used to recover from pulmonary fibrosis and long Covid that you will live even one day longer. But I can promise you that, while these methods and guidelines that I've followed may not add years to your life, they will *add more life to your years*. You will be healthier, happier, and bring more joy to yourself, and the people around you.

I have also met folks on this pulmonary fibrosis journey who are absolutely miserable. They complain constantly about everything, and have a way of draining the energy out of any place they're in. It's sad to see folks so caught up in depression, dwelling on their poor health, when I know that they are one decision away from turning that around. The fact that you're reading this book indicates that you believe there is more living that you want to do. I felt the same way, and although I may never run a marathon again, or do an open water 2-mile ocean swim, I can travel once again. I am actively participating in life, I am not a burden on others, and I am contributing to life and making daily positive contributions to the people around me.

I decided to write this book at the insistence of medical professionals and friends, who saw the severe decline of my health to near death. They witnessed my recovery, which they called miraculous, and urged me to do something with it. This book won't make money for me - it is costing me $15,000 out of pocket to publish, so it may not even break even. However, I am pledging 25% of the revenue from the book to the Pulmonary Fibrosis Foundation, to fund awareness and research for PF.

While others may call my recovery from near death miraculous, I see it as a series of baby steps over the course of a year. Extremely difficult, but highly rewarding. Everything suggested in this book, I have tried personally. These are not just ideas and suggestions I read in another book or saw on the internet. If I haven't done it, it's not in this book. This book is about "adding life to your years, not just more years to life" which was the motto of The American Gerontology Society in 1956.

If you are reading this book, it's likely that you already get this concept, and you already have some optimistic view of life. However, if this book was given to you by some well-meaning relative or friend who wants you to change your attitude about living and health, then they have seem something in you that merits you giving the suggestions here a try, and what do you have to lose?

I have attempted in each chapter to provide a reasonable amount of medical science-based reasoning for the chapter topic. Then I will describe how I applied this knowledge and the results I have experienced. A year ago, my health had declined to the point that I was actively evaluating assisted living facilities to move to, and now I am planning a trip to Europe and have joined Pickleball and golf leagues.

Prior to January 2020, I was an Ironman Triathlete at the age of 62. I led a very active lifestyle of running, biking, and swimming every day, while also starting a new technology company as the CEO and founder. By January 2021 I was diagnosed with advanced stage pulmonary fibrosis, with enlarged nodules in my lungs, pulmonary embolisms, severe lung scarring, honeycombing of the lungs, architectural distortion of the lower lobes of my lungs, and only 30% lung function. I couldn't walk my dogs any longer and lived on five liters of oxygen 24 hours a day. Simply getting off the sofa to go to the restroom in my apartment would cause my heart rate to rapidly elevate, and I would become short of breath.

So, how did my health decline so rapidly? Let's go back to January 24, 2020. I was lying in my bed on the 13th floor of my condo, which overlooked the cruise ships in the Tampa Bay Cruise port. My body was wracked with aches, chills, fever, and coughing so violent my chest felt as if it was being torn apart. I had come down with some sort of flu, which I had never been prone to. The world felt like it was getting darker as I struggled to breathe. As the television news played in the other room, in the dim resources of my foggy half delirious, semi conscious state, I heard the CDC warning of a new, highly contagious type of flu that had come into the United States from China. Suddenly a bell went off in my head as I remembered the crowded Amtrak train car I had been in just four days prior. The train car was filled with 15 or 20 Chinese tourists that were storing their bags while I passed through during an overnight train trip in Florida. Being the friendly neighborly type I smiled and spoke to the folks there, and helped them stow their luggage.

As I heard the CDC warning, I thought of this, but quickly said to myself "no, that can't be. It's just a coincidence." In

January, 2020, the general public knew next to nothing about COVID-19, but I couldn't get that train out of my head. Two days after the train ride I came down with body aches, fever, and a cough, and now I could hardly breathe. More on the sickness stages later. For now, a little about me and why I'm writing this book.

A little about my background:

I am a 65-year-old man with three children and two grandchildren, retired from a long and successful career. Professionally, I have been in the information technology business for 40 years as a global executive and CEO of multiple large and small companies. At the age of 50, I realized my 255 pound power-weight-lifting body was not the best vessel to ensure a long, healthy life, so I made significant changes and became an endurance athlete. I began running, swimming, and bicycling, and started to race short triathlons. After several years of training, I had reduced my weight to a lean, muscular 185 pounds. I raced the Ironman Triathlon, which is a 2.4-mile swim followed by a 112 mile bike ride and a 26.2 mile marathon—all in under 17 hours. My best time for these races was 13 hours— decent for my 54-year-old age group.

I'm not a physician, nor a medical professional, but I would venture to say I know more about nutrition science and the power of nutrition, exercise, breathing and meditation in healing the causes of disease than the average medical school-trained physician. They are highly schooled in disease management using the pharmaceutical-centric approach to treating disease. Modern medicine has become more about disease and symptom management than about disease prevention and true healing.

Health and fitness have been my hobby since the age of 22, when I first began a lifelong meditation practice. This book is written from my personal perspective of health and wellness over 42 of my 65 years of life but focuses on how I have experienced reversal of a near death health crisis after contracting COVID-19, with Covid pneumonia, enduring long Covid, and ultimately being diagnosed with "end stage" pulmonary fibrosis.

My approach for my personal healing journey is the culmination of 11,000 hours of research and 10,000 hours applying these principles combined with over 15,000 hours of meditation. I have condensed my personal research from the thousands of books, research papers, medical journals and studies, podcasts and lectures, and I have described clearly what I've tried and what's worked for me. I present this as a guide that may also work for you.

Before undertaking the methods that worked for me, I encourage you to speak to your healthcare practitioner. Hopefully you have one who is open-minded and willing to collaborate and work with you in your health journey. I personally have had to fire a couple of physicians who were narrow-minded, lacked intellectual curiosity, and were entrenched in their own way of doing things through a single-minded pharmaceutical approach, unwilling to explore my well researched ideas. Here's an important disclaimer:

__This book is for general informational purposes only and does not constitute the practice of medicine, nursing or other professional health care services, including the giving of medical advice, and no doctor/patient relationship is formed. The use of information from this book, podcast or materials linked from this book is at the user's own risk.__

*__The content of this book is not intended to be a substitute
for professional medical advice, diagnosis, or treatment.
Users should not disregard or delay in obtaining medical
advice for any medical condition they may have and should
seek the assistance of their health care professionals for any
such conditions.__*

A little background that sets the stage: I was born in a small
town of 600 people in rural South Carolina, with working
class parents who lived through the depression era. I had a
normal, healthy childhood, learning the value of hard work.
I held a job starting at the age of 12, but still spent my days
running barefoot in the creeks, dirt roads, and fields of a
farming region of South Carolina. I worked on farms, in a
gas station, painted houses, and worked on shrimp boats.
After leaving South Carolina and moving to Dallas, TX, my
eyes were opened to all that the world had to offer.

I am one of the original biohackers. At the young age of 21,
while living in Dallas, Texas, studying an eastern metaphysical
religion, my eyes were opened to the great new possibilities
in the world beyond the small-minded humble upbringing
of the rural South.

I had watched my mother be medicated with tranquilizers
and pills, with more pills to counteract the side effects of the
rest. She was an early patient of Librium and Valium in the
1960s. I watched her brain being scrambled, and witnessed
her live a life of anxiety, worry, and fear as a result of the stack
of medications that the country doctors prescribed. I also
watched my father decline rapidly as a hard-working man
with ongoing breathing problems, which were diagnosed
as emphysema. He was without hope, according to the
doctors, who said that he would progressively get worse.

The only medications they offered were an asthma inhaler, and a periodic steroid shot of prednisone when his breathing became so bad he was unable to function.

I was tired of seeing sickness in my parents, who were only in their 50s and appeared much older., So as a young man, I began to explore new ideas such as isolation tanks, ozone generators for my apartment and herbs from the local farmer's market. I was captivated in 1980 when I read one of the original health food "bibles", East of Eden, by Jethro Kloss. I learned about herbs, bought them in bulk, and made my own concoctions with a capsule filler I purchased from the herbal hippies at the farmer's market.

This was the time when I had left behind my hard-core partying days of the 1970s, smoking marijuana, drinking alcohol, snorting cocaine and dropping acid. I had moved to a life where I wanted my mind pure and clear. During those formative years in my 20s, I meditated every day for 30 minutes upon awakening, and I fasted for 24 hours on only water, one day a week. There was a period of growth and success as I landed a job in the newly evolving industry of computer technology, then married my childhood sweetheart of 10 years and began a family. Soon we had our first of three beautiful children, our family was growing.

Forward to Tampa in January 2020

In spite of the misery of the "flu", I simply dismissed it with the thought that if this was some new type of Chinese flu, then I'd get over it. After all, I typically never got sick, and I was an endurance athlete who trained daily for triathlons. Although 62 years old, I was in excellent physical shape. I swam 1000 meters every morning in the pool, ran sprints and longer distances daily, rode my bicycle all over Tampa rather than driving–I was the picture of health with high energy and a lean athletic body. Most people thought me to be barely 50 years old.

The day after hearing the broadcast from the CDC, I was a little better, but I still had a fever and a cough. Taking time to go to a doctor was out of the question, because I came from a family of working-class stoic parents who never missed a day of work in their life due to sickness. So, a few days later, I was back in the pool, swimming and walking my dogs, not quite as strong as before, but convinced I would quickly recover. My nutrition was reasonably healthy, I took high-quality supplements and vitamins, and I was on no medications.

After rebounding quickly, I suffered a relapse, with the fever and cough returning. Again, I fought it off with fluids, good food and moderate exercise, but I could tell something was wrong in my body. Food started smelling funny and eventually I just didn't smell anything. Nothing tasted good. I've always enjoyed good quality food and eating out, and as an intermittent faster, I typically fasted 17 to 19 hours every single day. I looked forward to that really good meal during my feeding window. I'd been living an intermittent fasting lifestyle for several years. As a result, I maintained a weight of 180 pounds on my 6'1" frame, and my body fat percentage was very low, at 10 to 11%.

As the headlines began to build in February with mask mandates, more CDC warnings and Covid infections rising, I observed it all with a knowledge that I probably had Covid, but there were no tests available at that time and it would be another 6 to 7 months before antibody testing was available to the public.

I was deeply involved as an entrepreneur and starting a new technology company that I was personally funding, and I had a team of people working for me that I had to lead, so I just trudged forward even though I didn't feel myself and I was unable to exercise at my normal levels. Around this time in late February, our condo pool was closed, as well as our workout room, and then the local gym, where I trained daily. Tampa, like many cities, was beginning to shut down, and became a ghost town. There was nowhere to go out and we were told to shelter in place. So I became more and more sedentary as a result, isolated on the 13th floor of my condo, looking down at the now empty cruise ship port. I conducted meetings over zoom calls and watched lots of television. My shortness of breath became worse.

My employees noticed that I appeared blue on the zoom screen for our daily calls. One of our team members was a part-time paramedic. He encouraged me to buy an oximeter to check my oxygen level. Once I did that, I saw that my oxygen level was in the mid to high 80s most of the time, and I was strongly cautioned about that and told to go to a doctor. My normal pulmonologist was not seeing patients face-to-face, so we scheduled a zoom call and she encouraged me to go to an emergency room for my breathing. I finally decided to go to an urgent care facility, because I felt so weak, and the cough was persistent. When I arrived, I was exhausted because I had chosen to ride my bike the 1-mile distance rather than drive. At the clinic, they wouldn't allow any patients to even come into the waiting room. Instead, we had to stand outside and talk to them through a speaker. After great difficulty in determining if my insurance card was valid even though I offered to pay cash, they finally discussed my condition and told me they couldn't help me because they weren't equipped to deal with Covid patients. They referred me to another location across town that could actually do a Covid test. I was too sick to trek across town, so I just rode my bike back home and sheltered in place.

Time passed. A few weeks later I was getting progressively weaker, and it was getting difficult to breathe and to do normal activities. I coughed incessantly. I had very little appetite, but my sense of smell was gradually returning. Finally, things were bad enough that I went to the Tampa General Hospital emergency room, where I was treated like a leper. I tried to explain to them that I didn't have Covid but that I had it weeks before. Nonetheless, they were very cautious about me, and rightfully so. After several hours, I was taken to a bed in the ER, examined, and given x-rays. They were particularly alarmed because my oxygen saturation was in the low to mid 80s. Anything below 95% is dangerous, and below 90% is normally time to call the paramedics.

After the examination and x-rays, I was diagnosed with double pneumonia. They gave me steroids, antibiotics, and an albuterol inhaler. I was told to follow up with the pulmonologist the following week. There was no Covid test done at the time, since I had already had Covid months before, and in spite of being a very well-equipped hospital, Tampa General did not have antibody testing in the mid summer of 2020. The steroids helped, antibiotics helped, and albuterol inhaler gave me some temporary relief, however the conditions I was staying in during the lockdown had worsened in my apartment, because for months I had a problem with mold, caused by a hot water heater pipes bursting and flooding. Maintenance was not done to alleviate the mold, because the Apartment building was understaffed during Covid.

I moved out of the mold in August and moved to Sarasota, Florida, to a downtown apartment where I could walk to grocery stores and restaurants. But soon after I went off the steroids, I began having breathing problems and weakness in normal activities, so that I could no longer walk to stores or restaurants. I had groceries and meals delivered instead. By November 2020 I was very sick, and I went to an urgent care clinic where I was diagnosed once again with pneumonia. Upon looking at the x-ray, the doctor said, "Your lungs are a mess." They were quite alarmed as well that my blood saturation oxygen saturation was 78 when I arrived. They wanted to transport me to the hospital, but by then the hospitals were full of sick and dying Covid patients, so I wanted to avoid that, and instead got the Z-Pak antibiotics, prednisone, and another albuterol inhaler.

In December, I returned to urgent care with low oxygen saturation. The physician, seeing my oxygen was at 80, referred me to a pulmonologist, who couldn't see me for over a month due to the large influx of cases. By the time I got to the pulmonologist, I could barely walk to my bathroom, and I lived on cough syrup to prevent the continuous coughing. In late January I saw the pulmonologist for about five minutes. He then turned me over to his nursing assistant to do the six-minute walk test. They saw that I was having great difficulty, and my oxygen saturation was at 80%, so they immediately put me on supplemental oxygen and ordered a CT scan of my lungs, as well as a full work up of blood tests.

A few weeks later, they called to inform me that I had pulmonary fibrosis, end stage. There was severe honeycombing and fibrosis of my lungs, as well as an architectural distortion of my right lower lobe, enlarged lymph nodes and a pulmonary embolism. I had about 30% of normal lung function. The combination of these factors indicated that I could be dead in 1 to 3 years without a lung transplant. This was a great shock to me considering where I had been prior to Covid. My pulmonologist recommended that I get a surgical biopsy so that they could determine the cause of the pulmonary fibrosis.

I couldn't get a good understanding of what a biopsy would actually do from a curative standpoint, and I don't blindly follow doctor's orders, so I began to do my own research. In my next appointment I told him I did not want a surgical biopsy because of the high complication and infection rate, and the fact that many pulmonary fibrosis patients found themselves in a worse situation after a surgical biopsy. I also didn't want to spend any time in a hospital on a ventilator, as would be the case with a surgical biopsy, because it was clear to me that many people who went into the hospital with a lung condition during that period ended up on ventilators and were leaving the hospital via the morgue.

Because of my refusal of that biopsy, I asked for a second opinion. I was referred to the Mayo Clinic in Jacksonville. I had my initial intake with them, and they indicated that I should travel to Jacksonville and plan to stay for at least a week for a series of blood tests, and other tests and diagnostics that had already been performed by my pulmonologist. However, they also wanted me to plan to have a lung biopsy, which would entail me staying another 4 to 5 days for recovery. I chose not to go that route and my pulmonologist was infuriated with me for my refusal of the biopsy. He had an arrogant bedside manner in terms of dealing with patients and I found it hard to talk to him because he didn't listen. Furthermore, he was at least 100 pounds overweight on his 5-foot five frame, sweating and wheezing whenever he came into the room, so he didn't exactly instill confidence in me. He referred me to another pulmonologist in Sarasota. However, they were quite busy and it was a couple months before I could get an appointment.

So I returned home did more research. I became weaker and in mid-2021 I began my "end-of-life planning". I did the normal Will and Living Will. Since I lived alone with two small older dogs, I began to arrange for their adoption by family members after I died. There were many nights in 2021 when I went to bed and and felt that there was a very real possibility that I would not wake up. I found peace with that through my meditation practice, and I was OK with dying. I had a friend who had died, and it was four days before anyone found him, so while I would be OK if I died, I didn't want my dogs to be in the home for an extended period of time with no one checking on them... I found an app for my phone called Snug, which I recommend for anyone who is older and lives alone. If you don't check in by 9 AM each morning, the Snug app sends an alert to five people on your list and contacts the police for a wellness check. This gave me comfort that my dogs would not be there alone for an extended period of time, and each night before I went to bed I would always check to make sure they had plenty of water so that they could make it the day or however long until people showed up for them. As I look back on it, it was a very sad and depressing time, being alone and preparing to die any day, but during the time it was occurring I was just putting one foot in front of the other and taking care of things that were necessary.

By November 2021, 11 months after the diagnosis of PF, but about 18 months living with PF, I had dropped from 180 pounds of muscular frame to 150 pounds. My once muscular physique dwindled away. I had a turkey neck, my chest was sunken, my legs and arms were skinny and weak. I was on 5 L of oxygen continuously and still struggled to maintain greater than about 93% saturation. I could hardly walk to the restroom, and I showered sometimes only once every two weeks because it was too exhausting. Due to oxygen anxiety, I couldn't close my eyes and put my head underwater without panicking. I paid dog walkers to come twice a day to walk my pets, I paid Instacart and GrubHub and Uber eats to deliver my groceries and meals. I had a housekeeper come in to do basic cleaning weekly. I walked only about 1500 steps daily with oxygen and would have to stop every 20 steps to take a 1-to-2-minute rest. My walking heart rate at that time with oxygen was 115 to 120, sometimes higher.

I lived in a four-story apartment in downtown Sarasota, and I couldn't even walk down the stairs to take my dogs outside, so I would have to walk a long way to the elevators which caused a panic attack due to breathing anxiety. I couldn't clean my house or even load my dishwasher, and when my groceries were delivered in bags to the door of my apartment, I had great difficulty just putting them in the cabinets, which would leave me completely exhausted. I was weak and dying. I did less and less and sat on the sofa 98% of my day.

My two dog walkers were caring young ladies, who told me about their father who had a bout with Covid and started seeing a nurse practitioner at a place called Latitude Clinic in Sarasota. Apparently, they had helped him improve greatly, and even get off oxygen supplementation. They persisted in suggesting I get help, but I didn't want to try a new doctor, especially because I couldn't get up and travel to a doctor's appointment. They contacted the doctor's office, who agreed to see me on a telemedicine zoom call. Their kind, caring concern for me beyond dog walking helped to turn my life around. Their description of their father's recovery was a ray of hope for me.

Finally, I agreed and had my video call with Ashley Dunmire, the nurse practitioner with Latitude Clinic. I supplied her with all my medical records by email and in my first appointment she actually listened closely and asked great questions. She had already reviewed my CT scans and bloodwork. After all that she said OK, based on our research and available treatment information, here's our long Covid and lung protocol. I felt an instant sense of relief, just the fact that they had a "protocol" gave me great comfort and hope. This was late November 2021, and in the charts of my health data at the end of this chapter you can see what a major turning point in my health and life that point was. I was initially prescribed budesonide, Singulair (or Montelucast) and Tessa pearls for cough, along with hydroxyzine for anxiety. We followed up in two weeks and she had done additional research and learned more about treatment using low-dose naltrexone for combating the massive inflation, inflammation and cytokines storm that Covid and long Covid is known to cause. Nurse Dunmire shared the research with me, knowing that I would find that kind of information important, and we started on that course.

In January 2022, a new CT Scan showed that in addition to the pulmonary fibrosis, I had another pulmonary embolism—a life threatening complication. My provider, Ashley Dunmire immediately contacted me to start me on Xarelto, a medication for this condition. However, I had no health insurance at the time, and the prescription cost was over $500 per month. Ashley contacted her pharmaceutical rep immediately, arranged to get two months of samples and a coupon for a free third month. Since I couldn't drive at the time, she then used her lunch break to drive 30 minutes to deliver me the samples so that I could start the medication immediately. What health care providers would even consider doing that?

The results of her medical care were immediate. I began to feel more stamina and a ray of hope, beginning in January 2022. I made the mental decision to fight for my life with everything I had. I knew that my sedentary lifestyle was contributing to my decline and so I hired a personal trainer to come to my apartment for workouts. She arrived, a young fit woman who could be a fitness model and found me wasting away. She looked at me with such pity, I couldn't walk down the stairs to our gym in the apartments. I couldn't do much of anything. She tried me on the stationary bicycle, but I could only ride it for maybe one minute before my heart rate rapidly accelerated my oxygen saturation plummeted, and I was near fainting. We tried for two weeks, but I had to let her go because it was just too frustrating. I knew what needed to be done since I'd trained and exercised most of my life, so I decided to put my own pulmonary rehab plan together.

I started by setting some goals for movement and steps on a daily basis that I would target and track on my Apple Watch, as I had for several years. Beginning in January 2022 I began making very slow progress, gradually getting from 1500 steps a day to 3000 steps per day. After a couple more months, I reached 5000 steps. I started using stretch cords to work my upper and lower body while I was still on 5 L of oxygen continually.

By around May, 2022, I began to feel stronger. I noticed I could take my oxygen off to take a shower without panicking. Additionally, I no longer was exhausted from minor activity. By June 2022, with my physician's concurrence, I discontinued all medications, except for low-dose naltrexone, and N-Acetyl Cysteine, which is an over-the-counter amino acid shown to have therapeutic effects on lungs. In the following chapters, I will list medications, herbs, and products I have tried, and what worked and what didn't.

I had sharpened and improved my meditation practice with twice daily deep meditations, and through that I no longer had anxiety. My lungs began to feel stronger due to the daily breathing exercises I was doing, and by July I could walk 8,000 steps every day with only 1 L of oxygen. My O2 saturation stayed above 97% while sleeping and awake. In July I joined the gym and began a more intense exercise program while continuing to use supplemental oxygen during the workouts and monitor my situation and heart rate continually. I knew from experience with the heart that we need to exercise it and elevate heart rate for periods of intensity, followed by recovery. I had trained this way for many years and knew the value of high intensity heart rate training. It was important that each day I would redline my heart rate through exercise into what I would call the yellow and red zone, meaning 85% percent of my maximum heart rate.

I began Noah Greenspan's Ultimate Pulmonary Boot Camp after reading Noah Greenspan's two books Guide to Pulmonary Fibrosis and Interstitial Lung Disease and Ultimate Pulmonary Wellness. The books are two I highly recommend for anyone suffering from this disease who desires more information about it. By August 2022 I was working out 6 to 7 days a week and I was riding my bicycle for short distances with oxygen. I began playing golf every week in September. I studied ways to strengthen my breathing muscles and the basic mechanics of breathing, which 99% of people do wrong, so I purchased an O2 Trainer™, which I learned of on a podcast interview of Bas Rutten, a world champion martial artist whose company sold the O2 Trainer.

The O2 Trainer device is the best I have found after trying several breath training devices. It requires and develops deep, powerful, diaphragmatic breathing through daily exercises, and it works like magic by really strengthening the diaphragm muscle. We live in a world of shallow breathers where for many people our lower, abdominal muscles are almost atrophied. I know from my illness and subsequent sedentary period that my diaphragm was not engaged in breathing. Rather, I was breathing from my nose and my upper chest.

The O2 Trainer retrained me to a proper breathing method. Within one week of starting the use of it, my spirometry measurement, which I had been tracking for nine months, showed a 50% increase in lung capacity (FEV1). This has been life changing. Soon I noticed that I could do without oxygen while at rest and still maintain a 98% saturation. A year ago, without oxygen I would have been in the 80 to 85% danger zone.

Here's what my days are like now: I wake up early without an alarm, check my sleep score on my Apple Watch, which shows me my sleeping heart rate, my oxygen saturation during sleep, the percentage of sleep in deep restful state, my heart rate variability, and the amount of sleep disruption I had. Next, I do a 10 minute mindfulness meditation followed by 10 minutes of Tai Chi. Then I do a 2 mile walk with my dogs, **without** oxygen. After coming home, I do some work on my company, and around midday I will have my single meal of the day. I go to the gym and work out for at least an hour. I'll come home and possibly ride the bike for another 30 minutes for 8 to 10 miles. During the work out at the gym and on my bike ride I still use oxygen supplementation at 1 L. I also occasionally play pickleball, and I take an afternoon walk of another 1.5 miles at the end of daylight. In my spare time I volunteer at the Salvation Army men's shelter. I have been trained as a hospice volunteer and I do work with the hospice, visiting patients in memory care Alzheimer's units, as well as working at the hospice house on Sunday mornings.

This book is written for you, the person with a diagnosis that means a significantly reduced life span, the person whose long term dreams are ostensibly being cut short with the announcement that the curtain will soon go down on this play—but you haven't finished! There's still so much you wanted to do. This book will show you a new hope for a full and amazing life, a life that can exceed what the doctors or medical papers forecast. This book is also for you, the caregiver, the person witnessing the lost hope and rapid decline of a loved one. This book is my personal manual of where I was and how I have recovered with new health and new hope. I hope you enjoy my story and if you apply to things that have worked for me, I hope that they will give you the quality of life that I have recovered.

Chapter Takeaways:

1. Do you want to live a longer and more joy filled life? Decide.
2. Don't be discouraged if you were not already accustomed to a lifestyle of exercise, it's not relevant at this point. What is more important is that you decide that you can recover your health and you begin to take one step at a time forward. It won't be easy, but the instructions in this book are clear and will get results for you.
3. *"It is easy to do what is bad and harmful to oneself, what is beneficial is supremely harder to do"*.

CHAPTER 2

Mindset: Sickness or Warrior?

It's Sunday morning at 8 AM, and I'm doing my volunteer time at the hospice house here in Bradenton, Florida. There are six patients and a frustrated nurse. They're understaffed and there are two patients crying out in pain, one doing what's called finger-painting, and no one is there to help the nurse. Apparently finger-painting is when a patient is playing with have their own excrement, delirious, and getting it everywhere. As I look at the list of current patients in the hospice house, we have 12 available beds. Yesterday there were nine patients here. Three passed away overnight, and there are six left. The ages of the ones who passed in the last 24 hours were 57, 80 and 84. The diagnosis of each was respiratory failure from Covid for the 57-year-old, the 80 year old died of end-stage pulmonary fibrosis, and the 84 year old had colon cancer. There it is, in neon lights, for me to look at end-stage pulmonary fibrosis and respiratory failure. Sitting thinking about this, and currently breathing without supplemental oxygen, I check my Apple Watch and it registers 98% Oxygen saturation. I take a breath of relief. This is after three hours without oxygen supplementation since I left home after my Tai Chi workout. A year ago, if I was off oxygen for ten minutes, even at rest, my saturation would have been low to mid 80s. I take a screenshot of my watch at 98% and savor the moment with immense gratitude. How did I get here from there? Stay tuned and I will describe how.

Today, around the world, 200,000 people will die—that's about two people per second. In the United States, according to the National Safety Council, the lifetime odds of death due to heart disease are 1 in 6 six; cancer, 1 in 7; Covid, 1 in 12; chronic lung disease, 1 in 28; motorcycle crash, 1 in 101; falling, 1 in 102; drowning 1 in 1024; choking on food, 1 in 2745; hornet, wasp, and bee stings, 1 in 57,825.

Interesting that Alzheimer's is not listed by the national safety Council, but in the US 121,499 deaths occurred from Alzheimer's in 2019. They make up 1/3 of the people in residential care communities, and Alzheimer's makes up 44% of hospice patients. 48% of nursing home residents are Alzheimer's patients. Two days ago, as part of my volunteer work with hospice, I visited a 93-year-old man who is a patient of a local memory care center in Bradenton, Florida. His daughter, who is a nurse, had asked that someone visit her father as she was very busy and unable to visit him in the center, and thought that he would do well with some outside company to talk to him.

The patient, I'll call him John, was a former triathlete and marathon runner, having run 800 races in his life. John was engaging in his conversation, although he didn't know where he was and would repeat the same sentences over and over. He did remember many of the marathons and we talked of our common history as triathletes, but he couldn't remember the last 30 seconds when we talked about where he was and what he was doing there. All around us in the memory care center were elderly folks wandering around, sitting in wheelchairs, or staring off into space. Several very old women were holding and caring for life sized infant dolls. Doll therapy is a common intervention for Alzheimer's patients to help address depression, agitation, and lack of fulfillment. It often gives dementia patients an anchor, a sense of attachment in a time of uncertainty.

As I think of the folks at the memory care center, who have a life expectancy of 7 to 10 years living in a world that seems very depressing, I wonder about the value of prolonging life in the face of such a debilitating disease. Compared to the life expectancy of end-stage pulmonary fibrosis of 1 to 5 years, I'm not sure which is better or worse. The simple fact is that we're all dying of something, and ultimately, we will all cross over from life to death, whether it's because we stepped in front of a bus while going to work, or cancer, stroke, heart disease, or pulmonary fibrosis. Life will end one day for each of us. Will we spend our remaining days on earth in fear of that ending, while clinging to life and using one possible medical treatment after another to prolong our lives a few more weeks or months or years?

Or will we transform our minds and go beyond the trite saying of "enjoy each moment" to a new place where we actually awaken to the present moment and its infinite beauty, immersed by the depth of the experience of life that words will never be able to aptly describe.

A little over a year ago, my mindset wasn't focused on the joy of life with a belief that the marvelous creation that is my body could be healed. In addition to many years of Eastern religious studies of Hinduism and new age metaphysical studies, I had a Christian upbringing, a deep understanding through study of the Christian Bible as a Holy Scripture, having been a teacher of adult Bible study. I enjoyed a sense of spiritual adventure. While working in the technology business and traveling around the world, I also worked part-time as a missionary in Africa, India and Jamaica, an international prison evangelist, preaching and teaching in prisons, conducting leadership conferences for pastors in India and Africa, as well as baptizing new Christians in Africa and in the Ganges River in India. But despite that background - all of that religious activity when I received my diagnosis of advanced stage pulmonary fibrosis, religion began to feel hollow to me. It became hard for me to believe that death would be so human-centric that I would simply pass into this place, called heaven, where there were earth-like buildings and temples and beautiful scenery and friends and streets, paved with gold. I was no longer buying that. It seemed so made up and simply a way to deal with death by putting a pretty face on it.

I struggled that year as I came to grips with my diagnosis of pulmonary fibrosis. I struggled in the confusion of what would come after death…was it just to be lights out? I had become bored with the many books and videos on YouTube about near death experiences, and testimonies of people who had gone down that tunnel into the light. It all just felt like our human minds were playing games and constructing ways for us to self soothe ourselves, in light of the fear of a "lights out" death. I had believed in my heart that I would live to be 120 years old, making it my goal, but was now facing imminent death. I felt like a boat that had lost its anchor, lost its mooring, and I was being blown about by the latest thoughts that ran through my brain.

After the diagnosis of end-stage pulmonary fibrosis and being put on oxygen in order to live, I grew more and more depressed. I developed a strong aversion to so many things in my life that I just wanted to hide from. I didn't want to get the mail for fear of overdue IRS tax notices, or any sort of bad news. I despised email because it was a constant reminder that the world of business that I had once found such great pleasure and purpose in, was now continuing along without me. Just months before, I had developed a new product to launch in the insurance industry and been very passionate about this latest technology start-up. But as the business got harder to launch, and I grew sicker, my co-founders and employees moved on to other interests, and I simply sunk deeper into despair and depression.

Self-medication with medical marijuana was one of the ways that I initially dealt with depression. Using various oral administration products, to avoid smoking or vaping due to my lung problems, I took marijuana daily to cope. But as soon as the high wore off, the depression and anxiety returned with a vengeance. Each day, and every evening. There's always been a part of me that did not want to be dependent on substances, whether pharmaceutical or otherwise, that would make me feel OK. I've spent most of my adult life not drinking or using any sort of recreational drugs because I didn't want anything to cloud my consciousness. I wanted to be clear, always.

My days in late mid to late 2021 were a repeat of the same dismal routine:

- Wake up around 7 AM
- Make coffee while sitting on a stool, because I couldn't stand up long enough to make it.
- Move to the sofa with coffee, put a blanket over my legs. I would cover up with a blanket and a

TV remote, and try to lose myself in some TV drama, binge-watching entire seasons of all sorts of television and movies. I'm sure I looked like a sick old man— I certainly felt like one.

- I'd order a Chick-fil-a breakfast bowl from Door Dash late morning, and mid-afternoon I'd order a taco bowl with extra carnitas or chicken. I thought I was eating healthy by choosing good restaurants, plus I was still taking 20 or so daily supplements. In retrospect I was committing nutritional suicide, killing myself with a diet rich in meat, sodium and low in whole food vegetables.

- The fast-food bags and garbage would pile up around my recliner because I didn't have the energy to take it to the garbage can. That was, after all, about seven steps I would have to make, and gradually I just continued to decrease all activity because I wanted to avoid shortness of breath and a racing heart. My body responded by continually declining in strength and health.

Since I couldn't walk my dogs without help, which came mid-morning and late afternoon, my dogs would urinate and defecate in an area of my apartment that I covered with Pet pee pads. During the night they would use them, and in the morning, I was too weak to bend over and bag the soiled pads, so I would simply cover them with new ones. Frequently I would have a stack of five or six pads with layers of waste in between. The dog walkers would sometimes help me clean up when they came by. Some days I would just sit and look at the mess and look at the dishes. I couldn't even find the strength to load the dishwasher, and would just feel more depressed, turn away from it all, and switch the TV on.

My deliveries of groceries, medication or other supplies would sometimes be dropped at my apartment mail room. Four floors down and about a half a block away, I would try for hours to motivate myself to go down there and get my packages. But most days I would fail, and I would have the dog walkers bring my packages up. This allowed me to avoid the journey of about 200 steps to the elevator, where I would experience claustrophobia and anxiety. Even if I was able to go downstairs, carrying an Amazon box back to my apartment was impossible, even with a cart.

Once in 2021, I didn't check my mail for three weeks. The postwoman finally brought it up to my apartment out of concern for me. I was experiencing the cycle that is spoken of so well in Noah Greenspan's books, where Noah describes how difficult tasks are avoided by pulmonary fibrosis patients. As a result, we begin to do less and less because things become harder and harder, so the less we do the harder even little things become. Even the smallest exertion becomes a monumental task. It's a death spiral and I was caught in it.

During the summer of 2021, I had tried a supposedly miraculous cure for lung and interstitial lung disease and breathing problems from the WEI institute, a provider of Chinese herbs. Their marketing was slick and promised a highly effective product. They clearly showed the herbs that were the core of the product, and how those herbs had a positive effect on lungs and directly affected the healing of lung disease. It was an expensive proposition - $3000 for a three-month supply. I bought it and it seemed to provide some immediate relief, but after a month or so it was clear nothing was changing. Perhaps that's because my mentality had not changed... I was grasping at straws, ordering various essential oils and home remedies for lung health, researching off label treatments and alternative methods to heal lungs. But two major problems remained: one, the end stage diagnosis was planted firmly in my mind, and with it, a three-year life expectancy gave me a vision of gradual decline to death. Two, I did nothing that would raise my heart rate and create fatigue, so I became weaker every day.

Taking a shower was a horrifying experience due to the extreme fatigue of getting in the shower and the oxygen anxiety of closing my eyes under the shower water, causing an immediate panic attack. My weight had dropped to 150 pounds, and my once muscular physique was replaced by a frame that I couldn't bear to see in the mirror, not wanting to see my visible ribs, my turkey neck, my skinny arms and legs.

I can't point to the exact moment or turning point, but somewhere in November 2021, something changed. Perhaps it was the loving attitude of Lesley and Veronica, the two sisters in their early 20s who walked my dogs. They were caring, compassionate, and they had genuine concern for me and love for my dogs. They would run errands for me and pick up medications and cough syrup from CVS, and sometimes deliver my packages. They had told me about the medical clinic in Sarasota that helped their father get off oxygen. Was this possible?

Up until that point, I had thought that the nasal cannula oxygen tank would be with me 24/7 till my death. Now there was this glimmer of hope that I might be able to live without it one day. After several promptings from Lesley and Veronica, I agreed to call Latitude Clinic, who was willing to see me on Zoom if I could send all my medical records ahead of time. After an initial video consultation I started on a new strategy. I believe the medication had a limited effect.

What changed for me was the revival of hope, and the care and collaboration I received from this new medical provider. I reawakened to my life experiences in which I had overcome seemingly insurmountable obstacles against great odds.

The power of vision and goals for change:

"A double minded man is unstable in all his ways."
James 1:8

To recover our life and health requires a single minded vision of success. The primary reason for all my accomplishments in life was my understanding the power of a long-term vision, and the power of setting goals and visualizing the achievement of them.

In my volunteer work with prisons and in transitional homes for men returning to society from prison, I saw a common problem: lack of any sort of vision of success. Most of these men had a career of multiple incarcerations and never had any sort of vision of themselves emerging from their current life. I greatly enjoyed teaching them the power of a vision of success and helping them to create plans to achieve things in their lives. I saw some men who were able to break free of the chains that had held them so long and realize success, find great jobs, start their own business and raise families.

I left college before graduating to go into business for myself, and I learned at an early age how to create a vision of success. This worked for me in every job and business that I undertook, all my life. Even without a degree, from the age of 28 throughout my career, I was in the top 1% of income in America. I made more money each year than most surgeons.

I had achieved much success in my life and by the age of 35 I had risen to the top of my profession as a global technology executive in the insurance business. I was was highly recruited by some of the largest companies in the world like IBM and General Electric. I flew over 5,000,000 miles in my travels for business. I took my family on vacations to Europe, Hawaii, the Caribbean, Mexico and all over the US.

We had a beautiful family - two boys and a girl - and I taught my children from a very early age how to meditate and how to visualize their goals. I taught them to write both short- and long-term goals and visions for their lives. One of my sons used these techniques of goal-setting and vision to become a star in collegiate and professional baseball. Even without the talent of most of his peers in baseball, he rose to the top through visualization, setting goals and hard work. He attended college on a full baseball scholarship. While in college, he set a goal to become the NCAA National Player of the Year in 2010 and to be drafted into major league baseball. In his college career he broke and still holds three NCAA records for the most career home runs, RBIs, and on-bases. In 2010, he was named the consensus NCAA National Player of the Year out of over 5000 collegiate baseball players. That summer he was drafted to play professional baseball by the Tampa Bay Rays. He credits his accomplishments to the lessons he learned as a child on the power of visualization, mindset, setting goals, affirmations, and holding on to a clear vision of success.

Another son became an attorney after graduating in economics from a major four-year university and he has successfully launched and sold two technology companies and has become a highly successful entrepreneur.

During my career in business, and in volunteer work in community service, I had created a seminar on the power of visualization and goals, and I taught this to Rotary groups, companies of my own and friends' companies with excellent results. Many peoples' lives were changed dramatically by establishing a big vision for their life and developing goals to achieve their vision. I taught these seminars in the US and Africa, in prisons, halfway-houses, and church leadership conferences. It just always worked.

These techniques enabled me at the age of 52 to transform myself from a 255 pounds overweight weight lifter into a 185 pound Ironman triathlete. By setting a vision and goals, creating the right mindset, and developing a plan, I had stood on the shore of the Irish Sea in Wales, England in 2011 along with 3000 other triathletes from around the globe and raced Ironman Wales. Six weeks later I raced Ironman Florida and finished with my best time ever of 13 hours and nine minutes.

With the illness of pulmonary fibrosis, I knew what I needed to do! My mindset had been completely wrong, and my vision was one of becoming an old man and dying soon. Something had to change, and it needed to start in my own mind. I could not wait on some magic cure from a pharmaceutical company or some miracle my doctor would perform. I decided this was a battle that I could and would win and I would do all I could to live a long, healthy, and active life, enjoying every day. I began to re-envision my future. I created a vision in my mind of hope and recovery in a renewed and long life.

Here's one trick I used to accomplish the seemingly impossible. It's easy and available to anyone. Almost everybody has some sort of smart phone with a calendar on it these days, and the power of scheduling a reminder to ourselves is huge. The reminders on my calendar are for more important things than appointments. I have used my calendar as a place for daily reminders of my vision and my goals and my purpose in life, and I've done this for many years. So first I sat with my journal and I wrote a vision for my life, then I created a set of goals that would lead me to that vision, and I built a weekly plan to follow. I put daily and weekly reminders on my calendar. I intended to hold onto a strong vision of recovery, and I knew it would require some fundamental areas of focus: working my action plan daily, breathing exercises, physical whole body exercise, high quality sleep, and the best nutrition I could possibly have. With this in mind, I began to prepare myself for a battle to recover from pulmonary fibrosis, avoid an early death, and emerge strong and active.

What follows are some of the calendar reminders that I use to help ensure I've got a strong vision, including goals and mindset notes that I am reminded of daily. **Calendar reminders can be scheduled daily or weekly and should be connected to goals. Reminders of what you intend to achieve each day or week.** When the calendar alert appears, it's a moment to visualize the goal and to affirm some important change and growth that you want in your life. For years I have set various recurring reminders with alarms to remind me of my purpose in life, who my ideal self is, and the values that I want to reflect in my life each day. Some reminders should be daily. Some should be weekly or biweekly.

I used this method to help me make the 180 degree turn from a death mindset in late 2021 to a mindset of life and health. Here are some of the important reminders I've used:

Calendar reminders:

Set the reminders as a ***recurring*** calendar event. So that I don't clutter the middle of my day when I may have actual appointments to put in my calendar, I set many of my calendar items and alerts for between 6 AM and 9 AM each morning. I will also set some reminders around noon because that's the time I want to reflect on how my day is going. I'll also set evening reminders so that I can gauge how my day went and reflect on the great things that happened that day.

Calendar item:
2022 I am healed completely & returning to enjoyable and creative work in 2023 for many more decades of earthly life. My vision of health, joy, purpose and mission is being fulfilled in many ways that I have imagined and more!
Friday, Dec 9, 2022
All day event
repeats every 2 weeks.

Calendar item:
Who is it that I wanna be? Look in the mirror and ask is that who I am?
Daily item at 7 PM

Calendar item
This is set for 8AM to remind me during my morning walk, it is an affirmation that I say out loud 15 times while walking: ***I bless my heart lungs organs and brain. Every day in every way I am better and better X 15 with immense Gratitude!***

Calendar item reminder for every day at noon taken from the book, The Four Agreements,
Be Impeccable with your word; Don't take anything personally; Don't make assumptions; Always do your best.

Calendar item for every morning at 7AM:
Current life purpose: taking charge of my life, my healing, and my destiny to demonstrate that seemingly hopeless illness can be healed with attitude, vision, blessing, mindfulness, grounding, nutrition, exercise. Taking this experience and message to others to set the captives free. Faith and action. Finding joy in each moment. Finishing well.

Weekly calendar item that I put on my calendar when I decided to write this book:
It is March 30, 2023 and I have sold my first copies of my first book: Recovering from Long Hall Covid and Pulmonary Fibrosis. The initial reviews from readers have been 5 Star and I am already being contacted to do interviews and podcasts about my journey of recovery

Calendar reminder weekly with training goals:
Breath training goals 2023 + Cycle 20 minutes on Level 7 @90 rpm w/o Oxygen +Swim 10 laps in the pool +Run .5 mile w/o Ox + Stair stepper 5 min w/o OS + Bolt score 35 current is 29

These are just examples for you, but they are very real reminders for me and there's quite a few more that I use and have evolved over time. I believe that this has been my **_superpower_** in healing and recovery, because each day I am reminded of

- where I'm going,
- the kind of person I want to be, and
- the kind of life I want to live.

By keeping these in the forefront of my mind, I live **_toward_** these goals, and it works, it just flat works.

As I've been involved in pulmonary fibrosis and lung disease support groups on Facebook, and other avenues, and I found there are so many people who are always waiting on something. They're waiting on their pulmonologist for an appointment to find out what the status of things are. They're waiting on a new CT scan or waiting on some possible new treatment. Some are waiting on a transplant. They are in paralysis mode. Nothing against transplants, but when my doctor suggested it, I asked how long a transplant would give me and he said maybe an additional 5 to 10 years. I thought about all that I would go through with the transplant, the new medications to prevent rejection, the various risks and dangers of the surgery, the long recovery, and the huge expense of a transplant, and I thought, "Why would I go through all that for another five years of watching Netflix?" I decided I would do my best to stay as strong and healthy as possible for as long as possible without a transplant and enjoy each day of my life rather than put myself on the "waiting list".

So many folks I see on support groups feel a sense of hopelessness and sadness, and they're oftentimes being sternly cautioned to not try anything new or different **_"without talking to the doctor first"._** **_Look, we all get that!_** *We don't* *want to be stupid, but why do so many people feel it necessary to repeat this mantra?* Even for things as simple as breathing exercises or walking I've seen people issuing these cautionary warnings.

The problem is that most folks I come across can't even ask their doctor a question because it takes weeks to get the appointment, and then some new test will be ordered which will take more weeks and then more weeks to for a follow up appointment which nine out of ten times is inconclusive. They're sadly caught in this limbo where they're always waiting and chasing the next possible medical event. In the meantime, they're missing life. They're missing this golden opportunity to stop the waiting game and get on with life whether it's a month a year or a decade remaining. They're waking up each day but not embracing the life that day offers. Rather, they're waiting on some future event that must occur for them to begin to live again.

The fact is, we're all dying of something. Earth is just one big hospice. 200,000 people will die today–most of them unexpectedly. We will all die eventually, but we have this moment, this day, to live, and so my decision was to make every moment count, become active and participatory in my life again.

One of the first steps I made to memorialize my mission of recovery was to send calendar invitations to some of my closest friends and family members to my birthday party. I sent out a calendar invitation by email, inviting them to my birthday **on January 18, 2058 which would be my hundredth birthday**. Next thing I did was put a picture on the lock screen of my phone of a Birthday cake with 100 candles on it. Then I began to calendar activities each day - affirmations and visions for health and life.

In the next chapter we will write your vision and goals and plans to put into your calendar. I hope you'll invite me to your hundredth birthday also!

Chapter Takeaways:

1. Our thoughts shape our reality. Change your thoughts, change your reality.
2. What's your mindset? Sick and dying while waiting on a cure? Or a **warrior** prepared to do battle against an early death?
3. Without a strong vision you may be just going through the motions.
4. The power of our words: our voice is the keyboard of our computer. It gives instructions to the brain and body and our body responds to what we say about it. ___Speaking sickness produces sickness; speaking health and vitality produce health and vitality.___

Chapter 3

Vision and Goals

You are at a fork in the road. You have a decision to make. Will you be a passive participant in your recovery? Will you wait weeks and months on your doctor's appointments and expect in that 5 to 10 minute period with your physician, they will somehow shed light on your recovery and perform some miracle of medical science to fix your physical, mental, and emotional state? Likely you will leave that physician's office disappointed, with no new hope or insight into how to improve your health, with no action plan other than to try a higher dose or a lower dose or a new pharmaceutical trial or get this new test scheduled. In the south we called this kicking the can down the road. You kick the can 10 yards, walk, and catch up to it, and you kick it again.

That's what doctor visits, tests and follow ups feel like in most cases. The new test will take several weeks to schedule, and two weeks later you'll have another follow up with your physician. Pretty soon two months have passed while you're waiting, waiting, waiting. You often feel paralyzed and unable to do anything but wait and ruminate on your miserable condition. If that sounds familiar, it's the plight of more than

3/4 of the people I talk to in pulmonary support groups on Facebook and Zoom calls.

The choice you can make is, will you decide now to take a highly active role in your health and recovery? If you are not committed to doing so, if you are not committed to taking steps to transform behaviors and significant areas of your life with exercise and a new approach to nutrition, *then stop reading right now and get a refund for this book.*

This book is not for people to load themselves up with more knowledge about possible methods for recovering from lung disease— it's about taking very specific actions to recover. Only you can do this. Your doctor, spouse, loved ones, or friends cannot. This book is my personal how-to manual on how I recovered from lung disease, but it was not easy. It was hard work, and there were uncomfortable changes that I had to make in my life, but it was worth it.

What an <u>active role</u> means:

Be your own advocate. This means you will use the vast resources of the Internet, YouTube, medical publications, support groups, and research that's available to you. As the table at the end of this book will show, there are at least 54 different approaches that I have tried, some worked, some didn't, but by no means do I know everything there is to know about lung disease, healing, and recovery. I do know far more than I did when I first was diagnosed. So I encourage you to search for what's working for others who have your condition, and look at what's new and emerging, what's tried and true, and what's been tried, but doesn't work.

A word of caution here, research means to look for **credible** reports based on medical science, alternative holistic medicine, and health and wellness tips and advice from **more than a single source**. Don't fall for the infomercials that describe miracle cures of some new herb or potion that has no documented empirical data to support it other than some anecdotes. Look for reviews of products, reviews of medicines and alternative cures, but look also at the reviews of these emerging products and be sure that the opinions that are being put forth are not by the people who are only standing to gain if you purchase the product. I.e.: look for objective third-party sources of information. I shouldn't have to tell you this but do your homework and don't just read one website and rush off to purchase a product without due diligence in your personal research.

Important note: Invest in your health. I will tell you about tools I've used that have made a huge difference for me. Some are inexpensive and some are a little bit pricey. I didn't have unlimited funds to spend on every sort of treatment, and during two years of my pulmonary fibrosis journey I didn't even have health insurance. I only recently became old enough for Medicare. I chose wisely where I spent my money, and for the most part my investments have paid off in my recovery.

One of the most important investments is a tracking device for your activity, exercise, and sleep. It may cost a few hundred dollars, but it is an investment in your health. Pharmaceuticals for IPF often cost your health insurance company tens of thousands per year. Most folks are not concerned because the amount out of their pocket is negligible, but people would naturally examine the efficacy in detail if the monthly cost of a prescription would cost them $5,000 from their retirement savings. That's not uncommon for new drugs on the market. Often these exorbitant prices are paid by insurance companies and people dutifully take the meditation hoping for a miraculous result. However, the results are minor if any, and the side effects can be very difficult and disruptive to a person's quality of life.

One example is a well-known drug that supposedly slows the progression of IPF. The medication is quite expensive, and since I didn't have health insurance it would have cost me several thousand dollars per month. I delved into the actual clinical trials and research studies, which were quite surprising. The actual data showed that less than 30% of the people get any effect from the drug, and those that do find that there is some moderate slowing of the disease, which is not qualified objectively in any way. Yet many people deal with a myriad of side effects from that drug that adversely affect their quality of life. *I have yet to find a good clinical trial that compared nutrition, exercise, and breath training against the top pharmaceuticals to determine empirically which methods slow the disease progression of pulmonary fibrosis more.* I was my own case study. Over the last two years my advanced stage pulmonary fibrosis has not progressed but has improved. My quality of life and lung function have both improved, and I have the data to prove it.

I read recently about a new Alzheimer's drug from a Japanese company that is purported to *moderately slow the onset of Alzheimer's*. It has been fast-tracked for FDA approval. But in looking at the data from the trials, the drug must be timed perfectly for only certain types of patients to receive a benefit, and the benefit is likely only some extra months of delaying severe dementia. However, according to a report, even though the drug managed to moderately slow onset of the disease, there were "safety concerns", with some patients experiencing "serious adverse events", prompting investigators to say further studies may be needed. The cost of the drug? $26,500 per year!

As is the case with the well-known IPF drugs, there seems to be something lacking in the approach. What's lacking is a holistic look at the patient's lifestyle and the implementation of behavioral changes that have been shown countless times to improve overall quality of health and life. Rarely does a physician do an adequate evaluation of the patient's overall nutrition, lifestyle and exercise habits, which have a great impact either with or without the pharmaceutical drug.

Please know that I am not opposed to pharmaceutical approaches to disease management, but too often that's the only consideration given by busy physicians who say, "Take this pill and let's see how you're doing after 30 days." I can testify to that from my own evaluation by three different pulmonologists. They wanted to do a highly invasive, risky surgical biopsy of my lungs, and put me on a medication to prevent progression of the fibrosis. I chose not to not allow a surgical biopsy, which infuriated my pulmonologist, and I also refused the medication since the results showed very little curative effect, with a host of side effects. The pulmonologists I saw never asked me anything about my level of exercise, or my nutrition habits, they didn't show me techniques or exercises for proper breathing, which affects oxygen levels greatly.

I was simply prescribed supplemental oxygen but never counseled on proper breathing techniques, or even how to properly use supplemental oxygen. They simply had the local oxygen company contact me, a technician showed up and gave me the equipment, showed me how to operate it, and disappeared after a few minutes with no real education about level of oxygen flow during wakefulness, sleep, or how to conserve oxygen in the tanks, when to use a portable concentrator, and if it would work for me. Nothing. I was just a number. Another drop-off of oxygen equipment on the delivery day for the technician.

To play an active role in your recovery, create your own list of emerging alternatives for treating your condition. For the latest emerging pharmacological products and cures, read the detailed reports on studies and determine specifically what percentage of people are significantly helped by the medical protocol. Understand the side effects, and how often they occur. Balance your views by looking at these two sides of the equation. As stated, with IPF I have seen medications that are FDA approved that only moderately help 30% of the people, yet over 50% of the people experience unwelcome side effects and one of these medications cost over $10,000 per month.

Working in collaboration with your physician

Maintain your list of possible treatments and benefits and before your next doctor's appointment, and do this:

1. Contact your physician's office at least a week before your appointment and inform them that you need to speak to the physician's nurse or assistant, to prepare for your appointment, and that you have specific questions and concerns that must be addressed. You want to send those ahead of time so that they are prepared to respond when you arrive for your appointment.
2. Then send the information by email to them in a numbered, easy-to-read list. That includes possible treatments for your condition and current problems you're experiencing.

3.   Include all specific questions you have regarding your current treatment plan, and the longer-term treatment plan. Don't overwhelm them with minutia and multiple pages of questions. Just narrow it down to the top 10 most important items.

4.   Then, three days prior to your doctor's appointment, call and confirm that they have received your list and it has been placed into your file. Request that the nurse review it prior to your appointment time because you want to ensure that there is time to cover all your issues while you are with the physician. Be very firm on this. Don't let the receptionist dismiss you without agreeing to put this in your file AND send a note to the physician's assistant or the physician about your needs.

5.   On the date of your appointment, carry two printed copies of your list. When you get into the examination room, go over the list with the nurse who checks your vitals before the doctor comes in. Provide one copy to her, but also make sure that you have it when the doctor comes in, and keep one copy for yourself. Ask the assistant or nurse to be sure the doctor has seen the list when he or she arrives, as you don't want to surprise the doctor, but you want them to have time to thoughtfully consider your issues and questions.

6.   When the doctor comes in to see you, be sure they have the list and tell them you'd like to go over that either before or after they examine you and ask their own questions. Do not leave the exam room until they have covered all the items on the list. If the doctor won't give you this consideration, then perhaps you should find a new doctor. Don't be a docile Patient who meekly allows the doctor

to talk down to them and brusquely dismiss their questions and ideas.

Doctors are human beings, they are not gods, and they make mistakes quite often. The third leading cause of death in America is **Iatrogenic**, which is *physician error, and kills 225,000 people annually in hospitals alone. If the data were available for outside-of-hospital deaths, it would be significantly more.* Physicians don't have time to do all the research necessary on emerging trends, and so often they can be very dismissive of things they do not know much about. Make sure that they have an opinion based on their own factual knowledge or their own research, otherwise ask them to review it and get back to you.

There are vast amounts of medical knowledge that have been fed into artificial intelligence computer systems to support healthcare, and much of what the doctors today do in diagnosing illness and developing treatment protocols is and can be done by computers and then administered by nurse practitioners and physician's assistants. Doctors are augmented with knowledge that comes from computer systems that are able to consume and digest millions of documents and reports that a doctor is simply not able to read. Don't look at the doctor as some high and mighty being that knows everything, because they simply do not, they are human. They should approach you as a patient that they want to work with, in partnership for your improved health.

I found a nurse practitioner who views my health and recovery as a partnership effort between us. She researches the questions I send to her by email. She responds over email between appointments, and she also does additional research into emerging treatments and suggests new ideas. It's very important that all of your physician's ideas are not simply pharmaceutical alternatives, but are in some cases alternative or holistic treatments and lifestyle modifications. Holistic medicine is an emerging field and simply treating disease with medicine is an old method of ***disease management rather than health management***.

As your own advocate and researcher, it's time to take the next step as an active participant in your health and recovery. It's time now to begin with the end in mind. It's time to establish a vision for your health in the future, and goals and a plan for you to follow. As mentioned, I have used these methods for decades to change my own life for the better, and I've taught my children, corporate and religious leaders, prisoners, ex-cons, sales managers, and sales people to follow the same method. I know it works.

This method is simple and requires about 35 minutes to an hour and a little bit of thought. It's easy to implement. It's guaranteed to change your life after you've completed the steps. You will absolutely feel a higher sense of control of your destiny, and a greater peace.

According to Stephen Covey's groundbreaking book on the seven habits of highly successful people, let's ***begin with the end in mind***.

First, read through this section one time so you'll understand what you're going to do. Once you finish reading through the section, set your timer, go back step one and give yourself 30 minutes to complete the entire section.

1. Picture yourself five years from now, and imagine, taking a deep breath, looking up at the sky, and relaxing, with a sense of immense gratitude.

Imagine saying out loud to another person these words, *"I am so amazed and grateful today. I have achieved a vision I set for myself five years ago. Five years ago, I wrote down my vision for the next five years and it has been achieved. I am living out that vision today. I am where I wanted to be in my spiritual, mental, relational, financial, and physical health. And I got here by starting with a vision of today"*

2. Now back to the present moment, draw a dot with six lines radiating out from it Like a star. The beginning of each line represents the number 1, and the end of each line represents the highest achievement, 10.

3. At the end of each of the six lines line write one of the following words:
    • Financial
    • Spiritual
    • Health
    • Exercise
    • Social/relationships (includes family)
    • Purpose

4. Now look at each one of those areas of your life. On each line, place a dot representing where you think you currently sit in that area, whether it be a 2, a 5 or a 7. For example, if you have too much debt, not enough income, place a dot on the financial line between maybe one and four.. Do this for each line. If on the health line you know that today you don't really exercise at all, give yourself a one or a zero. Now connect the dots and see what this star chart looks like. Is it symmetrical, like a wagon wheel? Or are all of your lines somewhere around five or six?

If so, that's balanced - it's a pretty small wheel. Your objective would be to have all the lines somewhere around an eight. That would make a nice, large, round wheel. If all the dots are close to the center, then you don't have a wheel, you have a hub, but that's something we can work with. Of course, if it looks like a perfect wheel and everything is a 10 then you can discard this book, you're perfect and you have no need to improve.

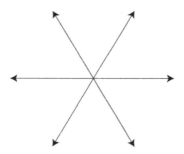

5. Now for each of the lines, think about what it would take to move the current rating to an eight or 9 or even a 10. For example, if exercise is only a 2, then what would it take to make it an 8?

6. Under your diagram, write the word exercise, put your current rating and write down what it would take to be eight or nine. For example, if today you don't exercise at all, while most authorities on health and wellness would suggest you need to exercise every day and do some rigorous training 3 to 4 times a week, then what will it take for you to get to that point? Write a statement that reflects that in the present tense FIVE YEARS FROM NOW, such as: ***I am in good physical health. I walk 8000 steps***

every day and I do yoga or strength training 30 minutes four times per week. That is a statement of what it would look like for you to rate an eight or nine on the exercise scale. For relationships and family perhaps, you rated a 2 today because you have no social interaction except Facebook, and maybe your children won't speak to you. To get to an 8 in the future, maybe you would say, "I am actively active socially with several neighbors and friends, and I talk to my children regularly about their lives."

7. Now, for each of these six areas, write the six PRESENT TENSE vision statements five years from now in a sentence. It's highly important for you to make these statements in the present, because we're not saying **what we want to do, we're saying what is already accomplished.** We're talking about what your life will look like five years from now in these areas. Now title the whole thing "My Five-Year Vision". This should take 15 minutes for you to complete.

8. Next, let's put down a set of 30-day goals for these six areas. Goals need to be specific, measurable, and achievable.

So, an example could be:

At the end of 30 days I will:

1. Relational and family. I have intentionally connected with two people socially through church community and speak to them regularly. I listen and learn and ask questions when I speak to others

rather than talk about myself. I have reached out to each of my children, and we are beginning to talk on a regular basis.

2. For exercise an example could be: I am walking each day at least 4000 steps and I am going to a gym or following an online strength training program and exercise plan twice per week. ***Remember, this is your 30-day plan. You don't expect to go from no exercise to six days a week of exercising 10,000 steps per day in just 30 days.*** Start slow and be sure that you inform your physician that you are undertaking an exercise program. Give them specifics as to what your plans are so that they'll know if you're trying to overachieve or doing too much based on your condition. ***There is no physician to my knowledge, except in rare cases of a patient's physical condition, who would say exercise is not good for you. Any physician worth their salt will tell you that some level of exercise is critically important for your health.

Once you have written your 30-day goal for each of the six areas, list these under your vision and put them on your calendar in a separate reminder, weekly.

1. Put your vision on your calendar and a weekly reminder also. Each week, take five minutes to review your vision, see it happening, and believe that you're capable of achieving that vision.
2. Then, on a weekly basis, look at your 30-day goals and rate how you're doing. Give yourself an A, B, C, D, or an F on your actions toward those goals.
3. And now for the final thing: have a weekly action plan. Know what you are going to do to move

toward your goals, put it down on your calendar, and make it a recurring event for seven days in a row. ***For example, tomorrow I will take two walks of at least 2000 steps each, and I will find and implement a strength-building plan using stretch cords, weights, or bodyweight exercise or in a gym***. Perhaps for your overall health you could put a goal to drink six glasses of water daily. I am avoiding sugar and eating a calorie restricted plant-based heart-healthy diet. For Spiritual, you could say that I am meditating each day for at least 10 minutes, and I am reading uplifting and motivational books or blogs to sharpen my mind.

Sample plan below. Make it your own and put it in your calendar. Review it weekly. With this you are moving toward taking control of your own destiny and being an active participant in your recovery

Sample Vision, Goals and Plan

Vision:

1. It is the year 2028 (this should be 5 years from the date you create your Vision).
2. My life and my health are better than I ever imagined it would be. I am filled with gratitude that:
3. My health is excellent, and I enjoy many activities and a rich active life with new experiences and adventures.

4. My resting heart rate is 15 BPM lower than five years ago and my walking heart rate is 20 BPM lower.
5. My weight is in perfect proportion to my height, and I enjoy varied daily exercises that keep me strong in my heart, lungs, muscles and joints.
6. I sleep soundly and restfully for 8 hours each night and enjoy waking up early with enthusiasm for the day ahead.
7. I eat a minimum calorie diet of many different healthy nutritious foods that give me energy and endurance.
8. My mind and my brain are sharp and I have an excellent memory.
9. I meditate daily, and consequently I have a peaceful composure about life; I live with ease and without fear or worry.
10. I have a good relationship with all of my family, and I talk to them frequently in uplifting positive conversations.
11. I have active social relationships and enjoy helping others and listening to them. I offer the wisdom of my advice only when asked.
12. I am debt free, live frugally, and I have all that I need in life.

Goals:

1. My 30-day goals are:
2. Complete a debt reduction plan and monthly budget.
3. Walk at least 5,000 steps daily.
4. Do deep breathing exercises every day.

5. Do strength training with a stretch cord or some type of resistance 3 days per week.
6. Meditate 10 minutes twice a day.
7. Go to bed each night by 10:30.
8. Monitor my calorie intake daily and plan my meals accordingly, with healthy, nutritious food.
9. Read and do puzzles or stimulating mental activities each day.
10. Contact an old or new friend to check in on their well being three times a week.
11. Contact a family member once a week to mostly listen to them and talk very little.
12. Find a way to volunteer my time to help others this month.

Daily Activity: examples

1. Walk two miles.
2. Meditate ten minutes.
3. Review budget
4. Review vision
5. Read weekly goals and give myself a letter grade for last week's goals.
6. Go to bed on time.
7. Don't eat after 6pm

Chapter Takeaways:

1. Going on a journey to a new place requires you to know where you are and where your destination is. Point A to Point D
2. Determine your Point A starting point by assessing your six life areas.

3.   Determine your destination Point D by writing your vision and goals.
4.   Create your roadmap reminders on a calendar to gauge your progress, keep the destination in mind always.
5.   Enjoy the journey.

Chapter 4

Activating Your Vision and Plan for Recovery

In order to make important behavioral changes, such as recovering from lung disease and restoring a healthy and active life, we must change our destructive behaviors and replace them with better ones. We must create new, healthy habits. According to human behavior economics, there are **four laws of behavioral change: c**

- **Cue**
- **Craving**
- **Response**
- **Reward.**

In his groundbreaking book, Atomic Habits, James Clear describes how to use these four laws in creating new habits.

1. First we need to *cue* the behavior, which means to make it obvious. Put the behavior prominently in front of your eyes so that it doesn't get lost in the distractions of life.

2. The second is to create a *craving,* which means to make it attractive. Ie: we want to feel or taste a good result from the behavior.

3. Third is a *response* to the craving, which means we need to make it easy to respond with a desired action.

4. And forth is a *reward.* We need to make it satisfying to have performed the behavior.

Long before Covid, I wanted to improve my swim for triathlons, because it was my weakest leg of the race. To do that I needed to swim regularly to work on stamina, endurance, and swim mechanics. Just one problem, I really hated swim training. I knew the best time of day to get it over with was early morning at 7 AM. However, I would invariably wake up, loaf around my home, and lapse into various distractions.

Even when I wanted to go swimming, I'd have to look around and find my goggles and my swimsuit, and I'd get distracted while doing that. So to follow the four laws and make it **obvious** I simply put my swim trunks and my goggles right beside my bed so that I would almost step on them when I woke up and be reminded of my commitment. Second, to make it **attractive,** I refused to have my thoroughly enjoyable morning coffee until I had completed my swim training. Going to the pool before coffee meant I had something to look forward to upon the completion of training—leaving that cold rooftop pool on the 23rd floor and coming down to my apartment to sit down with a hot cup of coffee. To make my behavior response obvious, I'd put my swim goggles and swimsuit beside the bed, so that I would immediately put them on and head upstairs to the pool. The **reward** was to make it satisfying, which meant that as I went through my swim training I was looking forward to completing it, knowing I would not only feel good, but feel like I really deserved that cup of coffee back in my warm apartment. This created a solid habit for me of swim training for 30 minutes every morning at 7 AM that lasted a couple years, until I caught Covid, and our pool was closed.

As you consider the behavioral changes that are necessary in terms of exercise, sleep, and nutrition, begin to think about ways to make these become habits. If you want to eliminate a bad habit, you simply use the reverse of each of these four principles. For instance, if you want to not eat brownies, you don't make them obvious, but rather you make them scarce by not buying them or hiding them so that you don't see them in the cabinet--you get the picture.

In this chapter we will use the power of your calendar and diary to activate your vision and make it real to you so that your life immediately begins to manifest your vision for health and longevity.

To get the most out of your vision and goals, let's look at a few principles extracted from well-known sources of life's wisdom, which happen to be scriptural references. Irrespective of your spiritual beliefs or religious practices, in all of the world religions and their unique yet often overlapping scriptures, we can find a golden thread of wisdom that is not tied to some religious doctrine, and in most cases can be tested empirically in science. Here are five principles that have served me well:

O *The power of life and death is in the tongue and they that love it shall eat its fruit. Proverbs 18:21*

○ *The tongue is like the rudder of a large ship that is small in size yet guides the whole ship. The tongue is like the bridle and bit in a horse's mouth, that, though it is small, it guides the large animal in its direction. James 3*

○ *When you pray, whatever things you desire, believe that you have received them and you shall have them. Mark 11: 24-25*

○ *Do not be anxious about anything, but in everything with prayer and petition, <u>with thanksgiving</u> present your requests to God. Philippians 4*

○ *We fix our eyes, not on what is seen, which is temporary, but what is unseen, which is eternal. 2 Corinthians 4:18*

So, in these words of timeless wisdom, we see several principles: the power of fixing our eyes on a vision, the power of our words in speaking life and health, or sickness and death over our body, and the importance of **gratitude** as an emotion of universal power. How do we give instructions to a computer? By the keyboard, right? Our lips, our voice our tongue are the keyboard of our brain and body. If we continually speak, fatigue, sickness, ill health, and we tell others all about our problems, then that is the programming that we are giving to our brain and body. In my life, I have seen this thousands of times, and the people I have encountered who just did not understand that they were speaking death and lack and sickness over their life over their finances over their children, and it was manifesting continually in their life.

However, if we speak words of life, energy, vitality, success and prosperity, and no matter what the circumstances are, we hold on to our vision speak words of life, then that's how we are programming our brain and body to respond. This has worked for me all my life for my own health and prosperity. *The power of life and death truly is in the tongue.*

Let's look at some ways to reinforce these principles in the way that we live our life.

Whenever we visualize a future outcome, think of it as a mold that is designed to pour melted plastic in to create some sort of figurine or statue. Visualization for us is like creating a mold in future space and holding onto that mold through our faith. By keeping it in the forefront of our mind, life fills that mold. It hardens and becomes reality. From 45 years of personal experience in visualization and achievement of goals, there is one secret I learned many years ago that is a **superpower** for achievement, and that is the added power of emotion. Not just any emotion. The most powerful emotion is a sense of gratitude for the realization and manifestation of the goal.

When I and my teams visualize outcomes, we have found that bathing the visualization in a *feeling of deep and expansive gratitude* is *practically a guarantee that the vision of the goal will manifest*.

Many years ago, my new wife and I were about to move across the country from South Carolina to San Francisco. Due to my new job and her current job, and the cost associated with flying back and forth, we couldn't really find time for a good house hunting trip for the two of us. We had to trust that I would fly out to begin work, take the weekend to find a good place to become our new San Francisco home, then we would move the following week. My wife was very nervous about this; naturally she didn't like the uncertainty of it. So, I used what worked for me time and again in my life.

I called her out into our backyard as the sun was setting, and put my arm around her. I said, "Close your eyes. Now let's picture standing in a place about two months from now in San Francisco. We're surrounded by beauty, we have a beautiful home, our pets are happy here and have room to run and play, and we have a view of San Francisco Bay. And imagine that we're saying to each other at that moment, this new home is perfect. We could not have found a better place to live. Imagine the feeling of immense gratitude that we will feel at that moment, knowing that today we created that vision and brought it to pass in our life."

What was the result? Three weeks later we were standing in a beautiful home on a hillside below Mount Tamalpais in Marin county California. In our large yard filled with fruit trees and a beautiful garden, we could see San Francisco Bay through the trees. We were able to remember how we visualized this moment with gratitude, and we were able to live in that home with the gratitude that we had imagined on that day. This is almost a law of physics in my opinion, and I have seen it work countless times in my life and in the lives of my children and others that I have worked with. *This practice will work for you in creating a vision of health and wellness, and a full, active life with many years to come.*

Here is a written abbreviated vision in my calendar as a weekly reminder:

2022 - I am healed completely & returning to enjoyable and creative work in 2023 for many more decades of earthly life. My vision of health, joy, purpose, and mission is being fulfilled in many ways that I have imagined and more! I am filled with gratitude for my recovery and restoration of health and I am taking this message to many people to give them hope and a plan of action for their own healthy future.

In the book <u>Atomic Habits</u>, James Clear describes an excellent way to build a new habit by using a habit you already do each day and then stack your new behavior on top of it, it's called habit stacking. Your current habit becomes the trigger for your new one.

One of my habit stacks is to combine my morning 2 mile dog walk with breathing exercises and affirmations. I use the final portion of my walk to do controlled exhales which we will discuss in more detail in Chapter 6. As I walk, I take a deep belly breath and then repeat the affirmation "Every day in every way I am better and better and better and better..." Using a slow, controlled exhale I try to say "better" as many times as possible, and sometimes I even sing it. This really empties my lungs with a full exhale which is highly therapeutic in recovering from lung disease. At night before bed I combine a breathing exercise after brushing my teeth and then sit down for a pre-bedtime meditation. Throughout the day I look for ways to stack good behaviors together to reinforce this pattern. It works "swimmingly" as the Brits say.

A **habit tracker** is a simple way to measure whether you did a habit. There are some good smart phone apps that help to track your habit and combine the results of your habit. In the exercise and sleep chapters we will look at the best apps I've used to lock in excellent health habits in my life. A simple basic format though is to use a calendar and cross off each day you stick with your routine. As time rolls by, the calendar becomes a record of your habit streak.

The comedian Jerry Seinfeld uses a habit tracker to stick with his streak of writing jokes. In the documentary Comedian, he explains that his goal is simply to "never break the chain" of writing jokes every day. In other words, he is not focused on how good or bad a particular joke is or how inspired he feels. He is simply focused on showing up and adding to his streak.

"Don't break the chain" is a powerful way to look at your new lifestyle change habits. Habit tracking is powerful because it leverages multiple laws of behavior change. It simultaneously makes a behavior obvious, attractive, and satisfying.

If you enjoy using apps on your smartphone to track your progress, an app I found extremely helpful was the Fabulous habit tracker, which is available for Apple or Android.

A fundamental of neurochemistry is that our brains have a built-in reward system. There are certain things that will release the neurochemical dopamine, which is the "feel good" brain chemical. When we do things that are in accordance with our desires and reach milestones of success, our brain releases little amounts of dopamine that reinforce our behavior and make us feel good. I discovered a few years ago that very small daily routines could give me a small dopamine releases throughout the day. Little things like making my bed, washing my linens, hand washing dishes rather than just throwing them in the dishwasher just make me feel good.

You may recall how your grade school teacher would provide an incentive for good behavior, or certain skills they want to build into your life. The incentive was often just a gold star beside your name. It made you feel good. That's a simple approach to how an app like Fabulous works. You put the habits that you want to build into the app, when during the day you want to accomplish them, and the app reminds you. Once you do it you get a gold star that celebrates your success. It may seem childish, but it works. It makes you feel good to know that you are moving forward and progressing in healthy behavioral change. Each day when I look at my HeartWatch app and see that I have achieved my goals of standing activity and exercise, it makes me feel good. I think that some mechanism like this to reward yourself with the simple knowledge that you are changing and becoming better is excellent.

There was a time when I rewarded myself via unhealthy behaviors, such as having a cocktail at the end of a hard day, or by using some medical marijuana after a particularly stressful morning of creative activities and meetings. Over time I realized these reward systems were hollow and unhealthy, and they ultimately resulted in a letdown. Today I get an muchj better feeling by just knowing that I have accomplished the healthy habits that I set out to accomplish that day.

For instance, the screenshot below is from the meditation app, Ten Percent Happier. It is an acknowledgment that I had completed an unbroken streak 52 consecutive weeks of consistent meditations. I know the life changes that meditation brought about in my health and my outlook and enjoyment of life, but this little award that was sent to me from the app made me feel even better. It was my badge of honor.

Similarly, my exercise tracking apps give me reports and summaries of my activity. I can look back 12 months or more and see a historic graph of how my exercise has gone up in minutes per day, and I can also view a graph that shows how my walking heart rate has gone down significantly. These things provide me visual reminders and a little bit of 'feel good' dopamine, and a confirmation that I am on the right track. I can't stress enough the importance of this type of good feedback that is available through technology.

If you don't use technology, find ways to keep a journal that will help you to look back on your progress and see the impact it's making on your life.

Below are three screenshots that show the value of using a habit tracker to see your progress. The Apple Watch tracks three fitness variables daily: exercise minutes, move calories burned, and stand minutes. The graphic view on the Apple Watch, or iPhone shows the three categories as rings, and your goal, each day is to <u>close your rings and leave no open</u>

rings. You're able to set your goals and increase them as you become stronger.

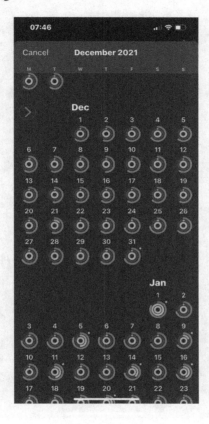

As you can see in the first screenshot from December 2021, my daily ability to close the rings was poor. The second screenshot shows a year later where I have consecutively closed all rings every month for about four months. Now it's a badge of honor. It makes me feel great to know I am consistent and progressing in my health. Don't underestimate the value of this type of tracking and the use of technology to make this tracking easy

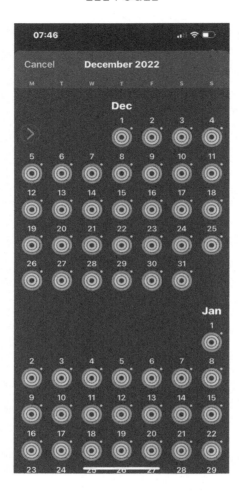

Summary of exercise minutes over the last year.

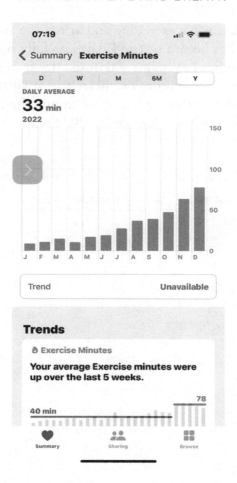

Results of increased exercise:

The following screenshots from the Apple Health app show the progress I have made based on increasing my exercise, and the result of exercise in lowering my heart rate and improving all of my biometrics. Notice the **precipitous decline i**n resting and walking heart rate that I have achieved through daily exercise. Heart rate is a universal measure of fitness.

the lower it is while exercising and at rest the stronger it is. Heart rate has been a metric I have carefully monitored in my recovery from pulmonary fibrosis. Invest in a heart rate tracker that will monitor your heart rate at all times Below we see that my resting rate has gone fromin the 70s in 2021 down to the low 50s in December 2022 with an average for the year of 61 BPM.

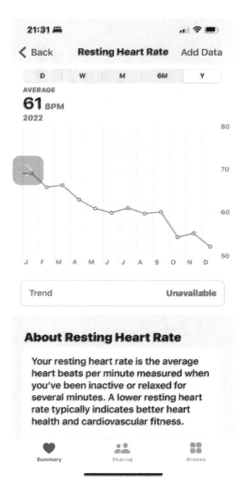

Walking heart rate decline over 12 months from **over 110 BPM in 2021 to the 80s by November 2022**:

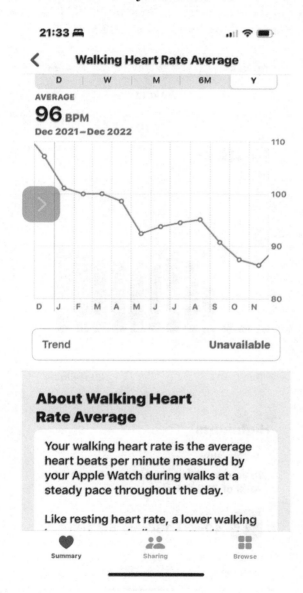

Monthly average exercise minutes over 12 months: This is what has strengthened my heart, from an average of 10 minutes of daily exercise in November 2021 to an average of over 2 hours daily by October 2022.

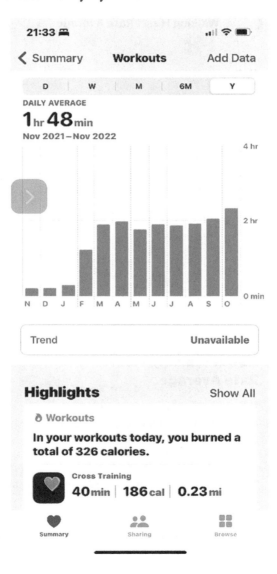

Chapter Takeaways:

1. Use the 4 Laws of Habit Change: Cue, Craving, Response Reward in order to create new healthy habits
2. To stop unhealthy behaviors, simply reverse the 4 laws
3. Stack new habits on top of regular daily activities
4. *Small changes done repeatedly create massive results long term!*

CHAPTER 5

Meditation and mindfulness for health and happiness

Chances are you woke up today with fear and worry about your condition. As a pulmonary fibrosis or other lung disease patient, or a Covid long hauler fearing the potential of your conditions deteriorating into one of these lung diseases. I know that feeling well. Our entire life can be consumed by our diagnosis. We wake up, with the oxygen cannula wrapped around our heads, concerned that we have become hypoxic while sleeping. We arise from bed, thinking about our oxygen saturation level and our first medications of the day that we need to keep our condition from worsening. We think about an upcoming appointment with our physician or a new test at the hospital or clinic or where we are on the waiting list for a lung transplant.

We may walk to the kitchen and fix a cup of coffee and sit down wondering what to do today. We may ruminate on our boredom with life, or our lack of purpose. For me, as a person who had spent so much of his life in an active leadership role in a high stress business environment, being in touch with people constantly, communicating with people by email, video conference, face-to-face, and telephone consuming

10 to 11 hours every day, suddenly I felt lost and without a purpose to live.

Even after COVID, before the pneumonia set in, my day typically began early morning reviewing emails from the night before, when others in distant time zones needed information from me. My day was normally booked with meetings as I reviewed the calendar and thought about how I needed to prepare for the day ahead. But suddenly all this activity came to a stop when my health began to deteriorate from long Covid and my first of many bouts with pneumonia. While it may seem like a fresh blessing after all the stress and activity of life, to suddenly enter a period where there is not a continual demand on us can seem disconcerting. After a while, we begin to feel a loss of purpose and value in our life. For me, my illness came around the same time that I reached retirement age and suddenly I felt old, sick and "out to pasture", no longer relevant as I watched young entrepreneurs starting companies, becoming successful while my latest entrepreneurial efforts languished due to my lack of strength and ability to continue to lead my fledgling company forward.

Certainly, this was a new season of life where, rather than dreading a full email inbox, I would scan my three inboxes for something that was a meaningful interchange with a common colleague, or former business contact, somewhere I was needed. But I would only find spam emails and offers to subscribe to the latest newsletter on health and aging topics. There was a great sadness accompanying this sudden inactivity. If this is something you've experienced, I can say this to you: the feeling of purposelessness and uselessness will go away. But it will come back again unless you take action to prevent this. There are lots of articles on aging and tips on making the most of your golden years, becoming involved in new hobbies and so forth, but being sick with a near term death sentence can tip the scales toward depression and feelings of worthlessness, in spite of the helpful daily articles from AARP.

That's the purpose of this chapter on mindfulness meditation. While I have spent much of my life as a mediator, in recent years it had been less of a priority due to the demands of work. In 2021, as I struggled through long Covid, I began a slow approach to re-energize my meditation practice using a couple of the well-known meditation apps at the time. I used Headspace at first, mainly because I really like the British voice of the teacher, always soothing, with whimsical graphics. I also stumbled upon the Ten Percent Happier app and found a couple of teachers that really made a difference in my new meditation practice. Joseph Goldstein, a well-known meditation teacher, and Sharon Salzberg, another teacher, and an excellent author of several books. Both really inspired and re-energized my meditation practice. They helped me to simplify it and truly enjoy it, and not look at meditation as a chore or an exercise that I had to do each day. As a result of the Ten Percent Happier app I really began to look forward to my meditation times.

Meditating consistently has helped me immeasurably. It has changed my life and become my greatest treasure and adventure in life. I'm also certain that meditation has helped to restore my physical health and my mental and emotional health. It has given me an equanimity, a calm composure that I've never known before. There is an unflappable, strong sense of presence and purpose in my life that is not easily influenced by external circumstances. I'm no longer buffeted by the winds of fear and worry about life, health, finances, and death.

In this Chapter I hope you will come to understand the many benefits of meditation:

1. Gaining a new perspective on stressful situations and building skills to manage your stress.
2. Increasing self-awareness.
3. Focusing on the present moment.
4. Reducing negative emotions.
5. Increasing imagination and creativity.
6. Increasing patience and tolerance.
7. Lowering resting heart rate. Overall improved physical health.
8. Greater happiness and resilience

Meditation has brought about so many profound changes in my life. It's never a chore, like some grueling exercise that I have to get through. It's the center of my life. It's a way of observing life in the present moment, aware of my thoughts and feelings and emotions, but not dictated by those thoughts, rather in control of them as the silent observer. It's as important to me as food and sleep. The more time I spend in meditation, the more that my entire life becomes one continuous meditation with the ability to observe all of life going around me, while I maintain equanimity, a calmness, like eye of the storm, centered and calm.

So what is mindfulness meditation? As defined by John Kabat Zinn, another well-known author and meditation teacher:

Mindfulness can be thought of as moment to moment, nonjudgmental awareness, cultivated by paying attention in a specific way that is in the present moment and as non-reactively, non-judgmentally and open heartedly as possible.

Why meditate according to health experts:

From the Mayo Clinic: https://www.mayoclinic.org/tests-procedures/meditation/about/pac-20385120

"Meditation may offer many benefits, such as helping with:

- Concentration
- Relaxation
- Inner peace
- Stress reduction
- Fatigue
- Emotional well-being

Research has found that meditation may help reduce symptoms of anxiety and depression, and meditation may improve physical health. For example, some research suggests meditation can help manage symptoms of conditions such as:

- Chronic pain
- Asthma
- Cancer
- Heart disease
- High blood pressure
- Sleep problems
- Digestive problems

Mayo Clinic Minute: Benefits of meditation

Stress, anxiety and a lack of sleep are problems that many people deal with every day. But there is one simple practice that can help: Meditation.

"Physically, people find they have improved mood, they sleep better, and have better memory and concentration."

Maria Caselli, a group fitness instructor at Mayo Clinic, says the benefits of just a few minutes of meditation a day can help, especially with stress.

"Meditation, which is the practice of focused concentration, bringing yourself back to the moment over and over again, actually addresses stress, whether positive or negative."

Meditation can also reduce the areas of anxiety, chronic pain, depression, heart disease and high blood pressure.

"The heart rate drops, your respiratory rate drops. There is decreased oxygen consumption, decreased carbon dioxide expired. The body is healing itself and starting to repair."

A 2018 analysis of 19 studies (1,160 total participants) found that mindfulness programs helped people lose weight and manage eating-related behaviors such as binge, emotional, and restrained eating. The results of the analysis showed that treatment programs, such as mindfulness-based stress reduction and mindfulness-based cognitive therapy, that combine formal meditation and mindfulness practices with informal mindfulness exercises, were especially effective methods for losing weight and managing eating.

A 2019 analysis of 29 studies (3,274 total participants) of mindfulness-based practices showed that use of mindfulness practices among people with cancer significantly reduced psychological distress, fatigue, sleep disturbance, pain, and symptoms of anxiety and depression. Most of their research and reviews show that committing to a daily practice improves the overall quality of life, and has long-term benefits for staying emotionally and physically healthy. Furthermore, studies show that meditation had similar effects as medications in treating depression, anxiety, and other emotional problems.

Are you a fault finder? Constantly judging what is wrong with the world or other people? What are the conversations that go on in your mind all day? Unforgiveness for someone that wronged you? Bitterness? Criticism? Doom scrolling through the news, politics and social media? Is there any doubt that this is unhealthy for you?

Much of life today is not mindful, but mindless. We are often engaged on auto pilot with a restless mind going wherever it wants to go, from thought to thought. It's as if we have no control over it. Long ago I heard a great quote that I have tried to live my life by and that is: *the mind is an excellent servant but a terrible master.*

Is there any doubt that this is unhealthy for you?

Meditation is not confined to a time when you sit quietly with the intention to meditate but can occur throughout your day as a you go about your life—it becomes a way of living that brings deep reflection on all of our life. It's a way to recognize the inner dialogue and just the recognition can help to change it. The use of "noting" in meditation the simple process of observing your thoughts and giving them a name such as "thinking, remembering, judging, hearing, fear, anger, etc". This process of noting our thoughts is a way to detach ourselves from the thoughts. Without detaching ourselves from the thoughts we become wrapped up and then we become them.

Scriptural wisdom for meditation

There is timeless, eternal wisdom for life in the Holy Books of many of the world religions. I personally have found the Christian Bible to be a tremendous source of wisdom for reflection and meditation. Here are two of my favorite scriptures that have always given me renewed hope and optimism in my life.

> "Therefore, everyone who hears these words of mine and puts them into practice is like a wise man who built his house on the rock. The rain came down, the streams rose, and the winds blew and beat against that house; yet it did not fall, because it had its foundation on the rock. But everyone who hears these words of mine and does not put them into practice is like a foolish man who built his house on sand. The rain came down, the streams rose, and the winds blew and beat against that house, and it fell with a great crash." Matthew 7:24-27

This was spoken by Jesus, and "these words of mine" that he references were simply his instructions for life that are contained throughout the scripture—words about love, compassion, forgiveness, and giving to others. The visual representation of the personal strength of a person who listens to these words and puts them into practice is a powerful metaphor.

I personally have experienced times in my life where I focused more on financial success, buying things and impressing others. I was failing to meditate on timeless eternal principles of what it means to live a good life, and I found that when the storms of life came, my personal "house" fell with a great crash.

I also have spent a good portion of my life meditating, thinking on, and putting into practice eternal truths, and I have felt the strength of my personal house stand firmly against the storms of life. Encountering personal sickness or the sickness of loved ones can be a fierce storm of life, and meditation helps one to build their house on rock—unshakable.

Another scriptural view of meditation:

> *"Blessed is the man who does not walk in the counsel of the wicked or stand in the way of sinners or sit in the seat of mockers. But his delight is in the law of the LORD, and on his law he **meditates** day and night. He is like a tree planted by streams of water, which yields its fruit in season and whose leaf does not wither. Whatever he does prospers." Psalm 1:1 NIV*

The Hebrew word for **meditate** literally means to *chew the cud*. It is an agrarian term used to refer to how cows digest their food. Cows have two stomachs. They chew the food in their mouth and swallow it. The food then goes into the cow's first stomach for further digestive processing and breaking down. Then the food in the first stomach is sent back up to the cow's mouth where it is re-chewed and swallowed again, this time going to the second section of the cow's stomach in order to squeeze out all of the moisture and nutrition. While the visual of this may seem a bit disgusting, you can see that this is a way for us to understand how to occupy our mind with healthy activities such as chewing on a bit of wisdom. How much of our day is often spent chewing on some sort of offense that we received from another, or chewing on a resentment we feel toward a person or institution or chewing on our fear of a progressing illness or health condition. We have a moment-by-moment choice of what we fill our minds with.

I really love this beautiful metaphor in Psalm 1, a "tree planted by streams of water, yielding fruit in season and prospering in all that we do". These words have given me life and energy and hope for decades. My life has truly borne fruit, and I have prospered greatly, as have my children. Every moment that we spend meditating on beauty, perfection, gratitude, love, service and goodness pays immense dividends long into our future.

Many years ago, a wise mentor of mine said, "Lee, people are like ketchup packets, and if you squeeze a ketchup packet in your fist hard enough it will burst and what will come out? Ketchup, right? So too are our lives, when life squeezes you to the point of bursting what comes out? Profanity, bitterness, hopelessness, anger? Whatever comes out is what you have filled yourself with".

Since hearing those words many years ago, I have endeavored to fill my life mind with good thoughts of hope, gratitude, prosperity, health, success and wisdom, so that when life squeezed me, I didn't spew forth anger and ill will, but hope, optimism, and goodwill.

Here's a life hack to help you find, focus on and fill yourself with all the good and positive things in life:

Put a reminder on your calendar for the end of each day to **"List three good things that happened today"**. I set this reminder for 8 PM each day and it changed me greatly. It put me in the mindset of needing to identify three good things that happened that day, so I spent my days remembering to look for something good in the moments of the day, making a mental note to remember it for the "test" later that evening. Some nights I would struggle to recall three good things, some days it was difficult to limit it to only three. It is a simple fact that if we spend our day looking for good it changes us from the inside out, profoundly. Try this, make a calendar reminder to do this for two weeks— you'll be hooked— it is life changing.

What's the difference between prayer and meditation?

I will offer a quote from an interview with Mother Teresa by the CBS News Anchor, Dan Rather. Dan asked her about her well known lengthy periods of daily prayer. He asked Mother Teresa *what she said to God,* to which she responded, "*I don't say anything. I just listen.*" So Dan's follow-up question was, "Well, then what does God say to you?"

Mother Theresa smiled with confidence and answered, "*He doesn't say anything, he listens.* **And if you don't understand that I cannot explain it to you**".

Oftentimes, prayer is either mindless repetition which may serve a purpose of building strength in the subconscious mind, or prayer may be beseeching our God for help on some important matter. There was a humorous scripture in the life of the Prophet Moses when he was leading the nation of Israel out of captivity and away from slavery in Egypt to the Promised Land. Moses found himself and over two million Israelites at the edge of the Red Sea, with Pharaoh's army bearing down on them, and nowhere to turn. Moses was crying out to God to save him and the people, and God spoke to him and said *"why are you standing there crying out to me? Stretch forth your hand and part the sea"*. As the Scripture says, Moses stretched forth his hand and the seas parted and the nation of Israel escaped on dry land.

Whatever your beliefs about scripture and the reality of examples like this, there is a timeless wisdom at work here. Rather than wailing and moaning to God about our problem, which oftentimes is simply restating and rehearsing the problem, making it seem larger the more we talk about it, why not take this moment to stop crying out to God to solve our problem and stretch forth our hand to **take action**. This to me is one of the most powerful examples of how prayer can be ineffective, or worse, we can continue to re-instantiate the conditions we're seeking to escape from.

This ties into our mindset in our visualization discussed in chapter 2. Visualization is creating a "mind movie". When you create a mind movie, you program yourself into that future situation, whether it's good or bad. My son who broke three NCAA baseball records for hitting, knew the power of those mind movies. He knew that if he went to the plate remembering the last time when he struck out, that movie playing in his mind, with fear to amplify, it would create a duplicate performance resulting in a strike out. He knew he had to delete that old movie and create a new mind movie of hitting the ball with power. This was his personal superpower enabling him to become one of the greatest collegiate players of all time.

Our experiences are emotionally charged. Whether it's a childhood trauma, a divorce, the loss of a loved one, or the person who cut you off in traffic today. In the original emotionally charged experience, our brain secretes neurochemicals that instantaneously flood our body, triggering a fight or flight, or stress response. In a more positive experience, there may be extreme joy, fulfillment and contentment.

Whatever the type of emotional event, the brain and our body instantiate a neurochemical environment that permeates our entire being. This is a part of our survival mechanism and it's wired into our DNA and the circuitry of our bodies. The interesting thing about this is that our brain really doesn't know the difference between the original experience and the mental reenactment where we recall and relive that experience. Our brain responds the same way, by reinstating the exact same release of the same neurochemicals in our body which creates the same negative stress response, fight or flight response, or the feeling of joy and contentment. This is why in chapter two we focused so much on what vision we hold before us and how we visualize our future self. We program ourselves to move into a life of health, contentment, prosperity, and joy.

But we all know folks who continue to talk about some emotional event or trauma that they just cannot let go. They live in bitterness, regret, shame, resentment, or other unhealthy emotional states. These emotional states serve to create disharmony in the body, mind, and spirit, which leads to poor health downstream. Each time you remember, rehearse, or talk about some stressful event, you are taking your entire being right back to that stressful event and creating the same toxic, unhealthy neurochemical body response as the original event. This is not just common sense, there are volumes of studies on how unhealthy that sort of mental rumination is. Many folks are stuck in the past, quite literally, because of their own mind movies. Stressful emotions are so powerful that we can become addicted to them. We become addicted to reliving the stressful event, even if it's a miserable, painful experience. We've all known what that's like, to not be able to drop some memory of an event that brings us shame, anger, or emotional pain, but we continue to relive it and replay the video in our mind—we can't stop thinking about it.

This is where meditation comes in. Beginning to step away from the event, create some distance by awakening as our true self, who is an observer of our thoughts and experiences. This is the first step in a good meditation practice. We are not our thoughts. But until we realize that truth and disengage ourselves from being swept away in our thoughts, then we **are** our thoughts—and our life reflects our thoughts. Once we realize we are not our thoughts and we take control of our mind, we begin to change the focus to a more positive mindset, a more optimistic, hope-filled view of our future. As a result our lives align to that vision. We realize that the trauma that happened is no longer happening, it's just a mental state, and we can observe it like a cloud in the sky.

Beginning or refining your meditation practice:

Here's a simple way to begin a meditation practice that removes some of the mystery and makes it practical.

Step 1:

Find a quiet place in your home where you can be uninterrupted for 10-15 minutes. It can be morning, afternoon, or nighttime. I meditate early in the morning and just before bedtime, but I believe if I were to only meditate one time per day, it would be morning since it sets the tone for the rest of my day.

Most teachers suggest that we create an anchor to settle our mind on, and I find that helpful. The most used anchor is the simple act of breathing. I prefer breathing as my own anchor in meditation. While we will cover breathing mechanics and how we should breathe in the next chapter, for now just follow these simple steps:

- Sit upright in an alert position. Your hands can be in your lap or on your thighs. Put a gentle smile on your face– it's amazing how well that facilitates meditation. A smile releases endorphins in our brain– another all-natural, organic, feel-good chemical.
- Gently close your eyes and allow your mind to focus on the sensation of breathing. Don't try to change how you breathe, but just breathe in your natural way and observe it.
- Find the place in your body where the sensation of breathing is clearest or strongest, whether that's

in the belly and diaphragm, the chest, the nose, or the throat.

- Begin to gently and quietly just observe the breath coming and going naturally.

- It's normal for our minds to wander continuously, so don't chastise yourself for that, but when you find that you've forgotten the breath completely and you are deep in thought about what you're cooking for lunch or the conversation you had last night with the neighbor, just gently return your attention to the breath. You're not doing anything wrong, it is completely natural for the mind to wander.

- A key part of the meditation process is simply to notice that the mind is wandering, which is the ultimate in mindfulness - to be aware of your thoughts rather than swept away with them. So if you find your thoughts wandering into some deep area 20 different times in a 10 minute meditation, and you have to return to the breath each time, that's OK. This is good mental training for you to improve your focus, concentration, and composure. Often our thoughts can create a sense of anxiousness, so rather than diving headlong into them, we want to return to a more neutral state in meditation.

- Just sit quietly like this, observing the breath for five to 10 minutes. You'll notice with daily practice it gets easier to focus your attention and just relax. See this time as your personal respite, the place where you go to be strengthened for the day, where you can get away from fears and worries and receive strength for the activities of life. View this time as sacred and nourishing for yourself, to prepare you before you launch into your day or go to sleep. Don't allow your meditation time to be a time of striving and condemning yourself for not getting it right. **<u>There is no getting it right and there is no getting it wrong.</u>** It's just sitting quietly and observing and getting in touch with that part of you that's always there, observing.

Whenever you think back to memories of your younger years, the memory may be like a picture or a video, but there was an observer who still observes that memory, that's the true, unchanging part of you. Feelings, sounds, sights, everything arises and goes away, but that central core part of us that's always observing is the only permanent part of us that there is. It's such a strong and freeing feeling to come in touch with that true self, which meditation enables us to do.

Step 2:

- As you become comfortable with practicing meditation in this manner, you will begin to see a pattern of quiet focus on the breath that is continually interspersed with thoughts flowing by. The thoughts are a continuous stream. No matter what you may think, it's impossible to stop the stream of thoughts, and it's unnecessary to eliminate this thought stream.
- Here is a way to not get swept away though by the thoughts in this thought stream. Pretend that your mind is a beautiful blue sky on a sunny day and the thoughts are like white fluffy clouds passing by in the sky. Clouds are always changing and moving and they never stay in one place. Clouds just like thoughts, are not solid. Clouds are just water vapor.

- As you observe your thoughts like clouds passing by, just notice them and watch for the next cloud to follow. It's a fun idea to put little mental labels on the clouds, for example you may be remembering an old memory, so make a mental note of this cloud as "remembering", you may see a cloud float by which is fear of death so note that cloud as "fear" and watch for the next cloud, you may see another cloud come along where you're anticipating going out to lunch with a friend, so note that cloud as "anticipation"

- As you begin to do this regularly you will notice that a cloud barely has appeared before it's replaced by the next cloud. There will be no shortage of clouds to observe in meditation.

- If you have flown on airplanes, you know that when you pass through a cloud it's difficult to see anything, and sometimes it can be quite bumpy. So too is the experience of going inside most of your thought clouds. You can get lost and bumped around in them. So instead of diving into the clouds simply "be the sky" observing the clouds from a distance and mentally noting what type of cloud it is: thinking, remembering, planning, anger, anticipation, dread, fear, hope. These are all feelings, that's what the clouds are. Don't try to stop the cloud and go inside of it, just make a mental note of the type of cloud, and then return your attention to your breath. The next thought cloud will soon follow, so simply note them, and watch them pass.

As you become more familiar with this method of observing your thoughts as passing clouds, you will begin to realize that ***you are not the clouds*** but that you are the observer of your cloudy thoughts. You are not the emotion of the cloudy thought, but you are the consistent observer of these feelings.

When you begin to see this and experience this viewpoint as the observer, it's a big breakthrough in your meditation practice. Most importantly, it's a breakthrough in your personal life. **When we realize we are not our thoughts, but we are this single point of awareness of our thoughts and feelings, this is amazingly liberating and strengthening**. This spills over into our daily life, creating a quiet, composed security in our permanent self— a stability of who we truly are. We realize that thoughts and feelings of sadness and joy, fear and worry come and go continually, but our true self, our awareness is always here. *It becomes our anchor in the storms of life, knowing who we truly are, as we observe life from a center of stability and consistency.*

Think back on a particular childhood memory, whether it was happy or sad, and look for your true self in the memory. You will realize that you were there, you were observing that moment, you were the one that was feeling that feeling. I enjoy mental games where I go back to memories of 50 years ago and look for my true self that was observing that moment. Realizing this solidifies our identity as the observer, as the one **unchanging** part of ourselves. The power that comes with this realization is immense. No longer do fear, worry, or anger consume us. We've always been here, we're still here, our lives have had millions of up and down moments, and will continue, but we are still here.

I learned something from a meditation teacher that I put on my calendar as a daily reminder, it follows here:

- Stop defining negative psychological mind conditions as a problem, simply be aware of them.
- When the mind is disturbed rather than asking what can I do about this, ask who am I that is aware of this?
- The center from which we are watching a disturbance CANNOT be disturbed.
- Awareness transcends that which it is aware of
- Unconditional happiness is a choice.
- The greatest gift that one can give to God Is to be pleased with his creation.
- We are using our will to resist one of two things: that which has already happened or that which may happen.
- It is not life's events that are causing frustration, stress and unhappiness, it is resistance to life's events that is causing it.

Here are four meditation apps for your smartphone that I've used and have found extremely helpful in my meditation practice.

Meditation Apps

App Name	Free Version Available	My rating
Ten Percent Happier	Yes	★ ★ ★ ★ ★
Waking Up with Sam Harris	No	★ ★ ★ ★ ★
Headspace	Yes	★ ★ ★ ★ ★
Calm	Yes	★ ★ ★ ★ ★

Happy trails along your meditation journey.

Chapter Takeaways:

1. In the words of the Star Wars sage, Yoda, *"try not; do"*. **Just start meditating.** If you feel you are trying to achieve some "state" or experience, don't. There is no way to get it wrong. Just sit quietly and observe, listen, and feel.
2. Even if it's just for five minutes as you begin your practice, do it daily and preferably at the same time. Regular time spent in meditation has a huge payoff in overall health.
3. To create the habit of meditation, stack it with some daily habit. Place it just before some activity you enjoy, such as breakfast or morning coffee. Initially this will seem like a "reward" for your meditation, but as the habit builds, the meditation becomes its own reward.
4. Meditation helps us notice things as they really are. It helps us connect to what is true in the moment and so much simple good insight comes from this.

CHAPTER 6

Breath of Life

With pulmonary fibrosis, the fibrotic scar tissue buildup in the lungs is considered a life-shortening illness with no cure, that gets progressively worse. There is, however, an absence of clear medical and scientific information on why the condition does get worse. As someone who has experienced the effects of pulmonary fibrosis, I believe that one key reason it gets worse is **inactivity,** and what I call "lazy" or **shallow breathing**. These two factors can actually compound themselves over time and cause the muscles required for healthy breathing to atrophy through lack of use.

Muscle Atrophy

One of the reasons that muscles atrophy in bedridden patients is that through a lack of use muscles lose tone and strength. The body is designed to move in order to stay healthy. If you allow your car to sit for long periods of time and rarely crank it or drive it you'll find the battery will die, the seals will dry out, and rust will build up on the parts that are designed to move. Our bodies are not much different.

According to medical science, muscle atrophy is when muscles waste away. It's usually caused by a lack of physical activity. Over time, without regular movement, your arm or leg can start to appear smaller, but not shorter, than the one you're able to move.

In some cases, muscle wasting can be reversed with a proper diet, exercise, and physical therapy.

A person who spends the majority of their time sitting will often find that their knees and joints become stiff. Calcium deposits and bone spurs begin to appear, causing pain when they do move, and their muscles become weaker. This makes movement more difficult, which leads to less movement, which leads to more difficulty when a person does move. If this pattern is not interrupted, a downward spiral to poor health continues, often quite rapidly. I experienced it firsthand with my lung condition. Similarly, a person who is hospitalized and spends time on a ventilator, and therefore does not use their breathing muscles, consequently experiences a degree of muscle atrophy in these important muscles associated with breathing.

What happened to me and many other patients with lung disease, is that we begin to depend on the oxygen that is forced into our lungs through a tank or concentrator via a nose cannula, and we avoid strenuous activity. Combine that with a sedentary lifestyle and we find not only our legs, arms, and back muscles weakening, but those important breathing muscles as well.

After my diagnosis with pulmonary fibrosis, I was prescribed supplemental oxygen, and at first it was such a relief to feel better after having been short of breath and hypoxic for almost a year. However, as I mentally dwelt upon the *supposed* shortened life expectancy of 3 to 5 years for an IPF patient, and I began to fiercely depend on my supplemental oxygen, my whole mindset changed quickly. I became afraid to spend even a few seconds without oxygen flowing through my cannula and I "saw" myself as a dying old man pulling his green oxygen tank on a cart.

As we discussed in an earlier chapter about the power of vision, it works both ways— positive or negative. My entire mindset and appearance quickly transformed to that mental vision of "old and sick". I went from a vibrant optimistic energetic 63 year old with an athletic, muscular body and a highly active lifestyle of running, swimming and cycling, to spending most of my time on the sofa, binge watching episodes of Yellowstone and Netflix movies. I had all my groceries delivered, and because I felt too weak to cook, I had UberEats, Door Dash and GrubHub deliver my meals from restaurants. On some occasions I even left the door to my condo unlocked so that the delivery person could bring my food to me in my recliner. When groceries arrived, it was an arduous effort just to put them away in the refrigerator and cabinets.

Over a period of months, my strong chest muscles withered and my chest became sunken. My 180 pound body shrank to an emaciated 150 pounds. My breathing mechanics became more focused on the upper chest and nasal area. I could hear myself breathe, and I was only using my nose and upper chest to take short "sniffs" of air rather than belly breathing deeply from my diaphragm. As a result of inactivity and poor breathing, I became progressively weaker, and the slightest exertion of walking to the bathroom or going to get a drink of water out of the kitchen would cause my heart rate to increase, and I would become short of breath and fatigued. When that happened, it triggered my stress response and I became more anxious and more hypoxic—leading to panic attacks and more rapid shallow breathing. It's a scientific fact that rapid shallow breathing lowers your blood oxygen saturation and disrupts the balance of carbon dioxide, which is not just a waste product but is vital in the balance of metabolism of your whole body. That is part of the reasoning behind the old home remedy for panic to breathe into a paper bag, because you would be increasing your carbon dioxide level by rebreathing CO_2, which would lower your anxiety.

Eventually I couldn't even take a shower because I was so weak that even removing my oxygen hose for a moment to wash my face in the shower would create oxygen anxiety, and I would panic. My shower became a claustrophobic tomb. Rather than taking a daily shower as I'd always done, I would shower once every week. Even though I was formerly an Ironman endurance athlete able to race continually for 12 to 14 hours of nonstop swimming, cycling, and running, I experienced the principle of "use it or lose it", and I lost almost everything, including my strength, health, optimism, hope, stamina and enjoyment of life.

Excessive Sitting is Beyond Unhealthy!

The importance of exercise has been drummed into our heads over the past 50 years, and for good reason. Getting regular exercise is one of the most important steps we can take to prevent and reverse disease, and we'll cover this in great detail later in chapter seven.

A growing body of research, however, has shown that *we don't get the full benefits of exercise if we're sitting too much.*

A study published in the *Journal of Applied Physiology*, found that "one hour of exercise failed to improve lipid, glucose, and insulin metabolism measured the next day in people that have been sitting for more than 13 hours a day."

Previous studies have found similar results. One showed that even marathon runners in training that are mostly sedentary outside of their exercise periods are at an increased risk of disease and early death.

Researchers have speculated that sitting for prolonged periods deactivates our metabolism and makes our bodies resistant to the beneficial effects of exercise.

This is an important finding since many Americans now sit for many hours a day.

Imagine someone that works at a desk for eight to nine hours, drives an hour to and from work, sits for meals, and then sits on the couch for a couple of hours watching TV after work— that's more than 13 hours of sitting.

The takeaway?

Exercise is important, **but so is reducing the amount of time you spend sitting.** As I write this book, I am standing up and dictating my manuscript notes into a mobile tablet device. I have retrained myself to spend as little time as possible sitting each day. My Apple Watch reminds me if I haven't stood in the last hour and I am quick to respond and stand and move around, whether watching TV, reading a book, on a zoom call or writing this book, I can stand and move whilst doing so.

Using a standing desk elevates the heart rate and may burn as many as 50 cal more per hour. If you stand at work for three hours a day that's the equivalent of 30,000 extra calories burned in a year, which is the equivalent of running 10 marathons!

Why is sitting around so bad for you? One reason may be endothelial dysfunction, the inability of the inner lining of your blood vessels to signal your arteries to relax normally in response to blood flow. Just as your muscles atrophy if you don't use them, "use it or lose it" may apply to arterial function as well. Increased blood flow promotes a healthy endothelium. Blood flow is what maintains the stability and integrity of the inner lining of your arteries. Without that constant tugging flow with each heartbeat of exertion, you can end up with arterial dysfunction diseases. What if sitting all day is part of your job? Research suggests treadmill desks may improve the health of office workers without detracting from work performance, but your office might not accommodate a standing desk. Preliminary evidence from observational as well as interventional studies suggests that regular interruptions in sitting time can be beneficial. And they don't have to be long. Breaks could be as short as one minute and not necessarily entail strenuous exercise—just walking up and down stairs may be enough.

In the book, *The Paleo Cure*, by Chris Kessler, the author recommends that we aim for walking about 10,000 steps a day and standing for about half of the day.

This might sound impossible if you work at a desk, but there are several ways to integrate more standing and walking into your day:

- Get or make a standing or treadmill desk. I simply use a small high top table I bought online for $40. It allows me to have an elevated work surface I can use while standing.

- Have walking meetings.
- If you take public transportation to work, get off a stop or two before the office and walk the rest of the way. Same thing on the way home.
- If you drive to work, park a mile away and walk to and from the office.
- Take the stairs, rather than the elevator or escalator.
- Whenever I enter someone's office and they tell me to have a seat, I simply refuse and find a place to stand. People are so habitual, they just sit in the car, ride an hour to the doctor's office, and now they immediately go sit down in the waiting room.

Every little bit of behavioral change adds up and pays compounded dividends. With a little bit of attention and ingenuity, you can significantly reduce the amount of time you spend sitting, improve your health, and extend your lifespan in the process.

The Deconditioning of our body and life

Noah Greenspan, a well-known pulmonary rehabilitation specialist, describes in his excellent book, Guide to Pulmonary Fibrosis and Interstitial Lung Disease, the downward spiral for PF patients quite well:

> "*As you become more deconditioned, one consequence is that your body does not use oxygen as efficiently. As a result, you then start to feel short of breath at lower levels of activity. Then, you start to avoid those (even lower level) activities, and so on and so forth. Again, this is called the dyspnea cycle or dyspnea spiral and our goal is to help you break that*

cycle by teaching you more effective breathing techniques—and teaching you how to exercise most effectively every time, so that your body becomes more efficient at using oxygen and you, more fit and less short of breath."

I am personally convinced that the major reason that pulmonary fibrosis is considered to be a progressive disease, is that people become less and less active, and then breathing muscles atrophy which then causes a lack of lung expansion that a deep diaphragmatic breath gives us.

This means that there are deep places in our lungs that become filled with scar tissue, like spiderwebs, often noted on CTScans as *honeycombing and ground grass glass opacities*. In my case the diagnosis showed this as well as an architectural distortion of the lungs. The architectural distortion was due to the scarring, which distorted my right lower lobe over time, as I used my breathing muscles less to expand my lungs.

When I began retraining my breathing muscles, occasionally on the deep belly breathing that expands my abdomen like a basketball, I would hear or feel something like a popping in my lungs. It felt like I was blowing up a balloon that was stuck together. It took a great deal of proper breath training, but eventually through exercise I began to feel my lungs and belly expand together. Gradually this allowed therapeutic breaths into the deepest part of my lungs.

Our bodies can survive on short, clipped breaths for many years, but that doesn't mean it's good for us. Over time, shallow breathing will limit the range of our diaphragms and lung capacity, and can lead to the high-shouldered, chest-out, neck-extended posture common in those with emphysema, asthma, and other respiratory problems. Fixing this breathing and this posture was relatively easy, however I have found that it must be reinforced daily through breathing exercises.

Now, with this basis of lack of proper use as a likely contributing factor of the "progressive" worsening of your lung condition, and the principle that as with all of our muscles and our brain we either "use it or lose it", let's undertake some techniques and methods to improve our breathing mechanics. Much of my research came from two books I read early in my journey with PF. They are <u>Breath</u> by James Nestor, and <u>Oxygen Advantage</u> by Patrick McKeon, which I recommend highly for those who wish to delve into the deeper science of breathing and the use of oxygen and CO_2 in our bodies for survival. I will quote both of these authors several times throughout this book.

A nation of shallow breathers

It's not just pulmonary fibrosis patients who develop poor breathing habits, but according to experts, we have become a nation of shallow chest breathers.

> *From Carol Krucoff's well researched article in the Washington Post:* <u>BREATHE - The Washington Post</u>
>
> *"Slow, deep breathing is probably the single best anti-stress medicine we have," says Gordon, a clinical professor of psychiatry at the Georgetown University School of Medicine and director of the Center for Mind-Body Medicine in the District. "When you bring air down into the lower portion of the lungs, where oxygen*

exchange is most efficient, everything changes. Heart rate slows, blood pressure decreases, muscles relax, anxiety eases and the mind calms. Breathing this way also gives people a sense of control over their body and their emotions that is extremely therapeutic."

Obviously, everyone alive knows how to breathe. But Gordon and other experts in the emerging field of mind-body medicine, say that few people in Western, industrialized society know how to breathe correctly. Taught to suck in our guts and puff out our chests, we're bombarded with a constant barrage of stress, which causes muscles to tense and respiration rate to increase. As a result, we've become a nation of shallow `chest breathers,` who primarily use the middle and upper portions of the lungs. Few people -- other than musicians, singers and some athletes -- are even aware that the abdomen should expand during inhalation to provide the optimum amount of oxygen needed to nourish all the cells in the body."

"Look around your office, and you'll see so little movement in people's bellies that it's a wonder they're actually alive," Gordon says. "Then watch a baby breathe and you'll see the belly go up and down, deep and slow." With age, most people shift from this healthy abdominal breathing to shallow chest breathing, he says. This strains the lungs, which must move faster to ensure adequate oxygen flow, and taxes the heart, which is forced to speed up to provide enough blood for oxygen transport. The result is a vicious cycle, where stress prompts shallow breathing, which in turn creates more stress.

"The simplest and most powerful technique for protecting your health is breathing," asserts Andrew Weil, director of the Program in Integrative Medicine and clinical professor of internal medicine at the University of Arizona in Tucson. Weil teaches `breathwork` to all his patients. "I have seen breath control alone achieve remarkable results: lowering blood pressure, ending heart arrhythmias, improving long-standing patterns of poor digestion, increasing blood circulation throughout the body, decreasing anxiety and allowing people to get off addictive anti-anxiety drugs and improving sleep and energy cycles."

"Unlike any other bodily function," he notes, "Breathing is the only one you can do either completely consciously or unconsciously. It's controlled by two different sets of nerves and muscles, voluntary and involuntary. And it's the only function through which the conscious mind can influence the involuntary, or autonomic, nervous system, which is responsible for revving-up the body to fight or flee."

"Western medical education at the moment doesn't include information of this kind," says Weil, who teaches breathing and other nontraditional techniques to what he calls `doctors of the future` through a variety of programs at his institution. "In the four years I spent at Harvard Medical School and a year of internship in San Francisco, I learned nothing of the healing power of breath. I learned about the anatomy of the respiratory system, and I learned about diseases of the respiratory tract. But I learned nothing about breath as the connection

between the conscious and unconscious mind, or as the doorway to control of the autonomic nervous system, or about using breathwork as a technique to control anxiety and regulate mental states"

At Duke University Medical Center in Durham, N.C., nurse Jon Seskevich has taught "soft belly breathing" to most of the more than 15,000 patients he's worked with since he became a full-time stress and pain management educator for the hospital in 1990. About half the patients he sees have cancer, and the others have a wide variety of ailments including heart disease, cystic fibrosis and lung disorders.

One of his most dramatic cases involved a lung cancer patient. "I walked into the room to find this very large man literally fighting for breath," Seskevich recalls. "His pulse oxygen was 74, and you want it to be 90 or above. I sat down next to him and started talking in a calm voice. I asked him if it was okay if I touched his belly. He nodded, so I put my hand on his belly and told him to breathe into my hand, to let his belly be soft and to let his abdomen rise into my hand."

After about six minutes of this, the man's pulse oxygen was 94 and he was breathing comfortably. "I didn't tell him to relax," Seskevich notes. "All day people were telling him to relax, and it seemed to make his struggle worse. I just told him to breathe softly into his belly. We didn't cure his cancer, but we may have saved him a trip to the intensive care unit"

Proper breath training

Let's start proper mechanical breath training by envisioning a couple of mechanical devices. Your air conditioning unit has a filter to clean the air entering your home. Your car has an air filter to keep damaging dust and sand particles from entering the inner workings of the engine. The inner mechanical workings of the AC or car engine are what sucks the air in, not the filter. *The filter is a <u>passive</u> barrier that restricts and concentrates airflow and cleans the air coming in.* Our nose in principle is the same type of filter. Our mouth is not. I repeat, the mouth is not an air intake aperture. You wouldn't have a separate air intake that circumvented the filter on your car or AC—that eliminates the purpose of the filter. The air is no longer concentrated and filtered.

Our body's air filter is the nose—a marvel of creation:

In a single breath, more molecules of air will pass through your nose than all the grains of sand on all the world's beaches—trillions and trillions of them. These little bits of air come from a few feet or several yards away. As they make their way toward you, they'll twist and spool and they'll keep twisting and spooling and scrolling as they pass into you, traveling at a speed of about five miles per hour. What directs their path are the turbinates, the six maze-like bones (three on each side) that begin at the opening of your nostrils and end just below your eyes. The turbinates are coiled chambers like a seashell, which is how they got their other name, nasal concha, after the conch shell. Mollusks use their shells to filter impurities and keep invaders out. Our nose does that for us.

The opening of the nostrils are covered in a mucous membrane, —*cells that moisten and warm incoming air to your body temperature, while simultaneously filtering out particles and pollutants.* Most of these particles could cause infection and irritation if they got into the lungs so the mucus is the body's **"first line of defense."** Like a miniature garbage collection truck, it collects inhaled debris in the nose, then moves all the junk down the throat and into the stomach, where it's sterilized by stomach acid, delivered to the intestines, and sent out of your body.

Working together, these areas of the nasal turbinates will *heat, clean, slow, and pressurize the air so that the lungs can extract more oxygen with each breath.* This is why nasal breathing is far more healthy and efficient than breathing through the mouth. The nose is the gatekeeper of our body.

So remember this: **First and foremost, noses are for breathing and mouths are for eating.**

Nasal breathing ensures a number of health benefits:

- Prevents dehydration of mouth and body.
- Filters air.
- Warms air.
- Reduces the heart rate.
- Creates nitric oxide for the lungs to open airways and blood vessels.
- Increases air pressure to take oxygen deeper into the larger lower lungs.
- Reduced lactic acid as more oxygen is delivered to working muscles.

A little-known fact about *right and left nostril breathing* from <u>Breath</u> by James Nestor:

> *"The right nostril is a gas pedal. When you're inhaling primarily through this channel, circulation speeds up, your body gets hotter, and cortisol levels, blood pressure, and heart rate all increase. This happens because breathing through the right side of the nose activates the sympathetic nervous system, the "fight or flight" mechanism that puts the body in a more elevated state of alertness and readiness. Breathing through the right nostril will also feed more blood to the opposite hemisphere of the brain, specifically to the prefrontal cortex, which has been associated with logical decisions, language, and computing.*
>
> *Inhaling through the left nostril has the opposite effect: it works as a kind of brake system to the right nostril's accelerator. The left nostril is more deeply connected to the parasympathetic nervous system, the rest-and-relax side that lowers blood pressure, cools the body, and reduces anxiety. Left nostril breathing shifts blood flow to the opposite side of the prefrontal cortex, to the area that influences creative thought and plays a role in the formation of mental abstractions and the production of negative emotions."*

Mouth Taping

Not necessarily for your talkative spouse! If you snore, have sleep apnea or wake up with a dry mouth and throat, there is a technique that I and thousands of others have used to ensure that we don't breathe through our mouth while sleeping. It's called mouth taping.

There are many YouTube videos on it, and most are entirely too complicated. It's really very simple, and since I first began doing it a year and a half ago, my sleep has improved dramatically, and I wake up feeling very refreshed each day.

All anyone really needs is a postage-stamp-size piece of tape at the center of the lips— placed over the center of the top and bottom lip. This method feels less claustrophobic and allows a space on the sides of the mouth if you need to cough or talk. The best tape I've found is the blue 3M Nexcare Durapore "durable cloth" tape, an all-purpose surgical tape with a gentle adhesive. You can find it at Walgreens or on Amazon. It is comfortable and easy to remove. When you wake up in the morning simply stick your tongue out and it pushes the tape off your lips. One of the first times I tried mouth taping, I used duct tape and pulled the skin off my lips trying to remove it – bad idea.

I was diagnosed with mild sleep apnea during a sleep study many years ago, and I was prescribed a CPAP machine. I could not tolerate the device with the hoses and noise while sleeping and found it highly disruptive to my sleep, so I never used it. Early in my journey with pulmonary fibrosis two years ago my physician once again wanted to try a "new and improved" CPAP machine on me and once again it completely disrupted my sleep. All my life I have awakened with a dry mouth and throat, sinus congestion and a bloody nose. I no longer need a CPAP, because since I've been taping my lips before sleep, I sleep more deeply, maintain 96% SPO2, never have a dry throat, and never have sinus congestion and bloody nose upon awakening—not to mention a postage size piece of mouth tape is much easier to wear than a CPAP.

An interesting fact about modern medicine's reliance on devices and medications to treat the symptoms rather than the cause is this. Over a 10 year period I have seen four pulmonologists, and not one has examined whether I am a nasal breather or a mouth breather. All four recommended a CPAP machine for my mild sleep apnea, but through my own research and focusing on nasal breathing by using sleep tape, while also losing some weight, my sleep apnea was completely cured.

Exercises and tools

Tools required:

- To track my lung function progress, I have used a spirometer, a digital **Peak Flow Meter** (available on Amazon for about $30, don't waste your money on a non-digital version, the digital is a little more expensive but consistently accurate).
- For the last two years I have measured and recorded my results, and the date of each test. The meter measures PEF (forced expiratory volume, the amount of air exhaled during the first second of a forced exhalation) and FEV1(peak expiratory flow, the speed of an exhale at maximum force after a full inhalation). This gives you a good reading on how well you are doing in terms of lung strength and recovery of lung function.
- I have seen an increase of over 50% of my lung volume through the breath training I have done. *In*

September 2021 my FEV1 was 450 and my PEF was 1.4 Liters. On January 5, 2023 my FEV1 was 625, and my PEF was 2.59. <u>That's a 39% improvement in FEV1 and an 85% improvement in PEF. This was accomplished by following the 7 Keys to Recovery that I have based this book upon.</u>

Pulse Oximeter: this is a simple device that fits on your right forefinger that measures your oxygen saturation—SPO2. I have owned several of these devices and my favorite, which seems to be the most accurate, is the Wellue, for about $30 on Amazon. It also comes with a lanyard so I can wear it around my neck while in the gym, in order to check my oxygen level during various workouts.

- While my Apple Watch will also record my SPO2, I find that having a good quality pulse oximeter gives me easier, more accurate readings if I am active. The Apple Watch requires you to be very still. It works great while sleeping, by measuring your oxygen at least once every hour and providing a record of that for you to review in the morning.
- Early in my journey with pulmonary fibrosis, I purchased a pulse oximeter, and I was shocked to see that my oxygen during any level of exertion was plummeting into the 70s. When my doctor at the emergency clinic saw this, they wanted to transport me to the hospital immediately. This was during the time of Covid, and the hospitals were full of more Covid than I wanted to be around, so I declined. A few months later I got my prescription for oxygen supplementation and saw that my SPO2 with oxygen would stay in the normal range of 95 to 100.

- But even today while working out in the gym, biking, or swimming under heavy exertion, my levels will drop into the mid 80s. Personally I do not worry about that since it's for a very short period of time, and the level recovers immediately upon completion of the exercise set. There are some schools of thought on fitness that believe that hypoxic training for a brief intermittent period is actually healthy for us. Prior to lung disease, while training for triathlons, I would do hypoxic sets in the swimming pool, where I would swim underwater without breathing as far as possible in repeated sets. My endurance gains were significant during that time, and I noticed that my heart rate continued to go down, indicating stronger fitness levels.

O2 Trainer™ this is a device that trains you to pinpoint and activate your most important breathing muscles: The diaphragm, abdomen, and intercostal muscles. It uses a system of resistance caps that range in size from 1 mm to 14 mm, in order to restrict airflow and cause resistance, thereby building stronger breathing muscles. The system comes with a very good instructional video and you should see significant gains in your lung function. The massive increase in my PEF came about within weeks of beginning my use of the O2Trainer. The device sells for $50-$60 on Amazon and is well worth the price. Since purchasing it five months ago, I have never missed a day doing the exercises with it. It only takes about three minutes a day to improve your lung function significantly.

Salt Breather: Salt rooms are becoming more prevalent in alternative health treatments, and my physician recommended

I find a salt room for its therapeutic effect on the lungs. Since I couldn't find a local salt room, I purchased a salt inhaler off of Amazon made by a company called Mockins. It is a $15 item and comes with Himalayan pink salt. I use this device daily for about five minutes. It does require you to inhale through your mouth, but I use it also to focus and train my abdominal muscles for massive expansion and for a complete lung emptying exhalation.

Exercises

- **Exercise1**: **Basketball Belly 4-7-15 count** Stand upright, mouth closed, and place your hands on the front and side of your abdomen. You want to be able to feel the movement of the abdomen as you breathe in. The idea is to feel your abdomen expand until it's round like a basketball. Forget the idea of holding your gut in, this is not a pose for a photographer! You want to really extend your gut like a beer belly. As you extend your belly it will naturally draw in your breath through your nose. Allow this extension to cause you to breathe in for a slow count of four, hold the breath in with your hands on your nice round belly for a count of seven, and then apply light pressure with your hands and let the air out slowly through pursed tight lips. Breathe out to a count of 15. As you breathe out you want to apply this light pressure so that you can feel your abdomen muscles and your diaphragm moving all the way back to your spine. This is a variation on a well-known exercise that's called the 4-7-8, and is my 4-7-15 version, since I have found that breathing out to a count of 15 ensures that I really focus on properly exhaling and emptying my lungs. I build "muscle memory" of what it feels like to press the diaphragm into the exhalation position. Do eight repetitions of this, once in the morning, and once before bedtime. Do it every day. This has been hugely helpful for controlling my diaphragm to get good inhales and complete exhales. Without a complete exhalation we are simply leaving stale air in our lungs and putting more air in on top of the stale air, often called air stacking. This technique is also excellent for calming and for pre-sleep relaxation— it promotes a sense of well-being.

- **Exercise 2**: use the **O2 Trainer** for 30 repetitions of the front abdominal muscles one day, and on alternate days 15 repetitions of the back breathing muscles. Follow the instructions that come with the device to get maximum results. Also continue to challenge yourself by increasing the resistance couch so that the muscles become stronger. After about a month I was using the smallest diameter breathing caps, which is a hard workout, for 30 reps, but it's made a huge difference in my lung function. There are many different types of breath training devices on the market, I have purchased at least five different ones prior to the O2Trainer, and none have made the significant improvement in my lung function that this device has. It is a small investment with a huge pay off in your overall health, in my opinion.

- **The Double Breath**: This exercise is one that helps you improve the capacity of your lungs to hold more air. It's very simple, you simply use your diaphragm and belly to take a large breath in slowly and once you've gotten that breath in pause and then take one more small breath and hold that. Then exhale slowly through pursed lips. This exercise helped me to break through some of the scar tissue that was restricting my lung capacity.

- **<u>Box Breathing</u>**:
  1. Breathe out slowly, releasing all the air from your lungs.
  2. Breathe in through your nose as you slowly count to four in your head.
  3. Hold your breath for a count of four.
  4. Exhale for another count of four.
  5. Hold your breath again for a count of four.
  6. Repeat for three to four rounds.

- **Walking affirmation with breath training:** Since you're either walking every day, or you will be as a part of this program, here's a technique I use each day that stacks two good habits together. During my walk I always ensure that I focus on breathing in for one step and breathing out for at least four steps. I also like to do affirmations that put me in a positive, hopeful frame of mind. One of my favorite affirmations is to say out loud every day, "in every way I am getting better and better." I've been using this on my return walk home each day for about nine months, and I typically say it 15 times. I also try to feel gratitude in my spirit as I say it, knowing that I truly am getting better and better. Recently as I focused on a more thorough exhale, I considered how singers must use a good inhale and a long exhale to sync properly, so I started singing my affirmation. I do it by taking a breath in, and then singing, "every day in every way

I am better and better and better and better and better and better and better." I try to say better as many times as possible, which forces me to control my exhalation much like a singer does. This little habit has become one of my favorite parts of my walk. My dogs don't think I sing very well, but it sounds good to me.

A Controlled Study of the effects of exercise on pulmonary function for idiopathic pulmonary fibrosis patients

There are mostly pharmaceutical studies available on slowing the progression of pulmonary fibrosis, but I recently came across a study that shows just how effective certain breathing exercises can be on improving lung function for patients.

The aim of the study was to investigate the impact of simple breathing exercises on patients with idiopathic pulmonary fibrosis. A total of 101 patients were verified and screened to participate in the study beginning in January 2015. The study measured lung function, chest x-ray, six minute walk distance, quality of life, an EKG at the sixth and 12th month of the trial.

Results:

- The exercise group showed improved quality of life score, improved lung function parameters, and improved six minute walk distance compared to the control group.
- No adverse events occurred in the exercise group.
- The incidence of acute exacerbation and one-year mortality were 7.69% and 2.56% respectively in

the exercise group which were significantly lower than those in the control group which were 20.9% and 9.3% respectively.

- At the 12th month of the trial, Ten patients from the exercise group showed increased lung volume on chest X-ray

- None of the patients in the exercise group had reduced lung volume at the 12th month of the trial. In contrast, 6 patients from the control group showed reduced lung volume

- The exercise group showed significantly less reduction in FVC than the control group The average 6-minute walk test was significantly greater in the exercise group than in the control group.

- The average reduction in FEV1 was significantly less in the exercise group than in the control group.

- The average reduction in DLCO was significantly less in the exercise group than in the control group

- Thus, FVC, FEV1, and DLCO were significantly improved in the exercise group compared with the control group.

Conclusion:

The RRPF Exercise program can delay the pulmonary function decline of patients with IPS and improve their quality of lif

New pulmonary rehabilitation exercise for pulmonary fibrosis to improve the pulmonary function and quality of life of patients with idiopathic pulmonary fibrosis: a randomized control trial - Shen - Annals of Palliative Medicine

The 3 LHP exercises:

LHP's RRPF includes the following 3 consecutive sets of movements (Figure S1):

(1). Deep breath of the whole lung. Patients stood upright, separated the two feet at the shoulder width, and placed both arms on the outer thighs. Then, patients raised both arms outward slowly and inhaled deeply till both hands closed over the top of the head. Subsequently, patients lowered both arms slowly and exhaled deeply till both arms returned to their original position. Patients repeated these movements 4 to 6 times within one minute (Figure S1A).

(2). Deep breath of unilateral lower lung. Patients stood upright, separated the two feet at the shoulder width, and placed both arms on the outer thighs. Then, patients raised the right arm outward slowly, bended the torso leftward to approximately 30-60° angle, and inhaled deeply. Subsequently, patients exhaled deeply and lowered the right arm to its original position. Patients repeated the movements using the left arm. These movements were repeated 4 to 6 times within one minute (Figure S1B).

(3). Deep breath of the upper lung. Patients stood upright, separated the two feet at the shoulder width, and placed both arms on the outer thighs. Then, patients crossed the two hands at the back of the neck, bended the head and neck forward, and exhaled deeply. Subsequently, patients kept the two hands crossed at the back of the neck, moved both arms backward, raised the head and neck slowly, and inhaled deeply. These movements were repeated 4 to 6 times within one minute (Figure S1C). During the breathing exercises, patients should make sure that the movements are done properly, but they should avoid overdoing the exercises. The exercises should be done step by step but not cause fatigue or exhaustion. If patients experience over- ventilation during the breathing exercises, then oxygen inhalation should be allowed.

Figure S1 Illustration of breathing exercise of LHP's RRPF. (A) Deep breath of the whole lung. Patients raised both arms outward slowly and inhaled deeply till both hands closed over the top of the head. Subsequently, patients lowered both arms slowly and exhaled deeply till both arms returned to their original position. (B) Deep breath of unilateral lower lung. Patients raised one arm outward slowly, bended the torso toward the opposite direction to the arm to approximately 30-60° angle, and inhaled deeply. Subsequently, patients exhaled deeply and lowered the arm to its original position. (C) Deep breath of upper lung. Patients crossed the two hands at the back of the neck, bended the head and neck forward, and exhaled deeply. Subsequently, patients kept the two hands crossed at the back of the neck, forced both arms backward, raised the head and neck slowly, and inhaled deeply.

Practice 2- 3 times Daily.

You don't have to do all these exercises daily, however I am reminded of asking my dentist if I needed to floss all of my teeth every day to which he responded, " Yyou only need to floss the ones you want to keep.".

A word about Oxygen and the importance of CO2

From the book <u>Oxygen Advantage</u> by Patrick Mckeon:

"The biggest obstacle to your health and fitness is a rarely identified problem: chronic over breathing. We can breathe two to three times more air than required without knowing it. To help determine if you are over breathing, see how many of these questions you answer "yes" to:

- *Do you sometimes breathe through your mouth as you go about your daily activities?*
- *Do you breathe through your mouth during deep sleep? (If you are not sure, do you wake up with a dry mouth in the morning?)*
- *Do you snore or hold your breath during sleep?*
- *Can you visibly notice your breathing during rest? To find out, take a look at your breathing right now. Spend a minute observing the movements of your chest or abdomen as you take each breath. The more movement you see, the heavier you breathe.*
- *When you observe your breathing, do you see more movements from the chest than from the abdomen?*
- *Do you regularly sigh throughout the day? (While one sigh every now and again is not an issue, regular sighing is enough to maintain chronic over breathing.)*
- *Do you sometimes hear your breathing during rest?*
- *Do you experience symptoms resulting from habitual over breathing, such as nasal congestion, tightening of the airways, fatigue, dizziness, or light-headedness?*

These poor breathing habits make the difference between a healthy and vibrant life and an ill and feeble one. Over breathing narrows the airways, limiting your body's ability to oxygenate. This constriction of blood vessels, leading to reduced blood flow to the heart and other organs and muscles. These systemic impacts will adversely affect your health, whether you're a professional athlete or your main exercise is walking up the stairs of your house. The lungs are the weak point—no matter how strong the rest of the body is—unnecessary, excess breaths take their toll. As most athletes know, our lungs give out long before our legs.

What determines how much oxygen your body can use is actually the amount of carbon dioxide in your blood. You may remember from biology class that we breathe in oxygen and breathe out carbon dioxide, also called CO_2. Most people believe that carbon dioxide is just a waste gas that we exhale from our lungs, but it is not. It is the key that allows the release of oxygen from the red blood cells to be metabolized by the body. This is called the Bohr Effect.

Most people don't realize that the amount of carbon dioxide present in our blood cells determines how much oxygen we can use and how we breathe determines the levels of carbon dioxide present in our blood. When we breathe correctly, we have sufficient carbon dioxide, and our breathing is quiet, controlled, and rhythmic. If we are over breathing, our breathing is heavy and erratic, and we exhale too much carbon dioxide. This leads to our body literally gasping for oxygen.

Chronic hyperventilation or over breathing simply means the habit of breathing a volume of air greater than your body requires. When we breathe more than what we require, too much carbon dioxide is exhaled from the lungs and, hence, is removed from the blood. It forces that door to a more closed position, making it harder for oxygen to pass through. Breathing excessively for short periods of time is not a significant problem, however, when we breathe too much over an extended period of days to weeks, a biochemical change takes place inside us that results in an increased sensitivity or lower tolerance to carbon dioxide. To counteract these bad habits, you must retrain yourself to breathe better.

Maintaining a correct breathing volume ensures that the ideal amount of carbon dioxide remains in the lungs, blood, tissues, and cells. Carbon dioxide performs a number of vital functions in the human body, including:

- Offloading of oxygen from the blood to be used by the cells.
- The dilation of the smooth muscle in the walls of the airways and blood vessels.
- The regulation of blood pH.

The only way to change your breathing volume and rate is by slowing down and diminishing the size of each breath to create a shortage of air. Optimum breathing, and all the health, endurance, and longevity benefits that come with it, is to practice fewer inhales and exhales in a smaller volume. To breathe, but to breathe less.

To be clear, breathing less is not the same as breathing slowly. Average adult lungs can hold about four to six liters of air. Which means that, even if we practice slow breathing at 5.5 breaths per minute, we could still be easily taking in twice the air we need. The key to optimum breathing, and all the health, endurance, and longevity benefits that come with it, is to practice fewer inhales and exhales in a smaller volume. To breathe, but to breathe less.

My experience

Using a pulse oximeter to measure my oxygen saturation has allowed me to experiment with different methods of breathing and the effect it has on my overall oxygen level. As I have practiced slower, deeper, but gentle breathing, I have found that my oxygen saturation actually increases the slower and easier that I breathe. I have found that sitting, leaning forward with my arms on my thighs is a good position for breathing lightly. This position also helps with coughing. If I lean back in a chair and press my back against a cushion or any surface, it tends to make me cough. Begin to take note of postural problems that may exacerbate coughing or your breathing patterns.

Here is a bit of trivia about the evolution of covering your mouth when coughing. People with pulmonary fibrosis call it the IPF cough. It's that nagging cough at night that doesn't bring up any phlegm but just feels like an irritation in your upper bronchial tubes. One of these problems that exacerbates and causes the cough to be a continual convulsive pattern is that when we cough, we over breathe through our mouth. The air is cool or polluted air that has not been cleansed, warmed, and humidified by the nose. I grew up placing my fist against my lips when I coughed so. In reality I am breathing in through my closed fist and coughing into my closed fist. This is actually pretty logical in that rather than opening my mouth wide and sucking in God knows what from the air around me, I am sucking in warmer air through my fist prior to the cough.

In recent years, we have seen the evolution of a new method of covering our coughing or sneezing where we cough into the crook of our elbow. We take the bend of the arm and put it over our mouth and nose. It has come to be known as the *"vampire cough"*, from the old movie images of a vampire covering his face with his arm. This method has evolved because coughing into our hand means that we expel germs and spittle into our hand and then touch surfaces or shake hands with others and spread those germs. Since we don't touch our inner elbows when greeting people and we don't use our inner elbow to open doors this evolution of the vampire cough is a nice change. It's important though that we hold our arm close to our mouth prior to the cough, which serves to restrict the airflow and to inhale warmer air from our body's warmth.

The "IPF Cough"

Have you noticed how certain foods or drinks will make you cough? Here's a simple fact that many people do not realize whatever food you put in your mouth, minute particles of the food or drink end up in your lungs. Of course, this is exacerbated by mouth breathers, but even for nasal breathers, the air flows down their throat from their nose can pick up particles of the food or drink they just swallowed, and these are aspirated directly into the lungs. That's why carbonated beverages, alcohol, and sugar create a cough, especially in people with sensitive lung conditions.

A tip about the IPF cough that I learned early in my journey is the effect of acupressure to stop coughing spasms. I discovered this from a pulmonary specialist on her YouTube channel, where she described key points that you can place pressure on using your fingertips, interrupting the coughing loop. When you can't stop coughing, place your middle finger of each hand into the area just below and on each side of the collarbone notch and press hard for about 10 seconds. This interrupts the signals to the brain that seem to be stuck in a loop when you have that convulsive, incessant cough. I have found that works immediately to stop the cough. Another location for acupressure is at the base of the back of the neck, on each side of the spinal column. Again, using a middle and forefinger to press hard into that area on each side of the spinal column just before it goes into the neck from the back. This location has worked equally well for me to stop cough spasms. Using these techniques, as well as adjusting my posture to prevent coughs from starting, has enabled me to forgo cough medicines completely since I began these techniques a couple years ago.

For much more science on breathing, lungs and optimal lung function I highly recommend Dr. Andrew Huberman's website Hubermanlab.com and his podcast episode https://podcasts.apple.com/us/podcast/huberman-lab/id1545953110?i=1000600532657

My conclusion about the effect of breathing exercises on lung function is evident in this book, however the empirical data below shows the actual improvement in lung function as measured by spirometer testing over a 12-month period.

Here is the table where I recorded my lung volume progress using the digital spirometer:

Date	PEF (normal range 530-602)	FEV1	Notes
9-2-21: 450	450	1.35	
9-11-21: 525	525	1.41	
2/21/2022	525	1.36	
2/22/2022	550	1.38	
2/27/2022	530	1.47	
3-1-22 AM	490	1.5	
3-4-22 AM	520	1.49	
3/12/2022	535	1.49	
3-15-22 (new mtr)	601	1.54	
3/16/2022	584	1.48	
3/16/2021	599	1.6	
3/18/2021	576	1.45	
3/22/2022	580	1.57	
3/25/2022	617	1.37	
3/25/2022	570	1.41	
3/29/2022	560	1.42	
4/18/2022	579	1.48	
4/26/2022	558	1.64	
4/26/2022	575	1.5	
5/3/2022	586	1.52	
6/15/2022	582	1.56	
6/15/2022	604	1.57	
8/3/2022	598	1.56	Began use of O2 Trainer
9/20/2022	543	2.32	
9/20/2022	570	2.07	
9/20/2022	553	1.76	
9/20/2022	568	2.13	
9/21/2022	517	2.31	
9/21/2022	546	1.9	
9/21/2022	553	1.91	
9/25/2022	563	1.79	
25-Sep	553	1.82	
25-Sep	526	1.96	
10/1/2022	552	2.16	
10/24/2022	568	2.13	
10/24/2022	603	2.12	
12-16-22	625	2.59	
1/5/2023	621	2.55	
2/4/2023	598	2.49	

Chapter Takeaways:

1. The breath begins in the belly! Not the nose or upper chest!
2. Nasal breathing is critical for your health.
3. Look down while eating to avoid choking.
4. Listen more than you talk; talking is one long exhale and causes overbreathing and mouth breathing.
5. Do the breathing exercises DAILY!

Chapter 7

Exercise

Interstitial Lung Disease (ILD) and Pulmonary Fibrosis (PF) are diseases in which there is reduced surface area in the lungs due to scar tissue, which restricts the lungs' ability to absorb oxygen from the air we breathe. This restricts the speed of oxygenation that the entire body requires for energy to move, think, and operate efficiently. If you're not familiar with the detailed structure of your alveoli and capillaries that transport oxygen, Noah Greenspan's book Guide to Interstitial Lung Diseases and Pulmonary Fibrosis, gives an excellent description of the lungs and how injury and illness affect them. Pulmonary fibrosis is often called IPF, which stands for idiopathic pulmonary fibrosis. Idiopathic means that we don't know the cause of the fibrotic scarring. Related lung diseases are emphysema, asthma, and COPD—chronic obstructive pulmonary disorder.

In normal lungs, there is a very thin membrane that allows oxygen to go from the airspace of the lung into the pulmonary capillary and the distance that the oxygen must travel to cross that membrane is very short. But with ILD, this membrane gets thicker and the distance for diffusion is longer, so the process is going to be less efficient, your pulmonary circulation is a series of parallel pipes. The entire volume of blood pumped by your heart, must travel through these pipes, and when we exercise, this cardiac output increases dramatically. In a person with normal, healthy lungs, there is enough capacity in the pipes to allow this increased blood volume to travel through the pulmonary circulation effectively. With an interstitial lung disease, there's inflammation and scarring in the gas exchanging part of the lung, so over time, you lose more and more of those pipes. If you lose enough of your pulmonary circulation, the red blood cells may have to go so fast during either exercise or activity, that they are unable to become fully saturated with oxygen by the time they get to the end. This is called exercise-induced oxygen desaturation, and the more capillaries you lose, the worse it gets, as interstitial lung disease progresses. People that have interstitial lung disease, may have oxygen saturation at rest that is normal or near normal, but during exercise, their oxygen saturation drops, often dramatically, and that's why they require large amounts of supplemental oxygen– to compensate for that impaired physiology. In summary if there are fewer healthy alveolar surfaces to get oxygen into our capillaries so that the oxygen can be transported to our heart and pumped to our muscles and brain which must have it, then our heart must work harder."

If our heart must work hard to get oxygen to our brain and muscles, but our blood vessels are constricted or partially blocked by arterial plaque, then our heart works even harder. That is why a complete physical by your healthcare provider is vitally important before embarking on an exercise program. **But don't delay, we must pay attention to strengthening our heart, so get a checkup immediately and get your doctor to agree to a moderate exercise program with a follow up with her in 30 days to report on your results.**

*One thing most medical professionals can agree on is that sitting on the sofa, watching the news, YouTube or Netflix **will not** strengthen your heart!*

Your heart and arteries are strengthened by a combination of exercise and very good nutrition. And by exercise I don't mean just short walks and ten minutes using a stretch cord, although that is likely where you will need to start from. We need to continually build from that. Most health and fitness scientists will agree that we need thirty to fifty minutes of good cardio exercise daily. Naturally, we start slow and build up gradually. But we must continue to exert ourselves more and more and get our heart rate into a higher zone that builds cardiovascular and pulmonary endurance.

In America, in spite of gyms and health clubs on every corner, and a culture of people who are avid exercise enthusiasts, we still have a major obesity crisis.

According to the Centers for Disease Control and Prevention, CDC:

- 73% of Americans are overweight or obese.
- 10% of those are classified as severely obese.
- Results of all this body fat is illness and premature death.
- Reducing calories is a part of the strategy, but by itself is not effective—our bodies just turn down the energy expenditure to conserve calories.
- *Weight reduction must be combined with exercise.*

For some of you reading this, you may not have a history of exercise as a part of your life. And so that you don't think I am some super great specimen of a lifelong practice of exercise, here's the fact. No matter what your situation is, starting an exercise program even very slowly and moderately at first is one of the most important decisions you can make to improve the quality of your life.

For much of my life I didn't really enjoy exercise, and I really hated running. In my 30s and 40s I began to lift weights and I took pride in my muscular physique, so I continued to lift weights heavier and heavier. I went through a phase when my sons were in their early teens that I wanted to show them how strong dad was! I got into powerlifting and at one point I could bench press over 400 pounds, but that was very hard on my body and joints. When I turned 50, I weighed 255 pounds, I was beastly strong, but aerobically I was weak. In order to live a long life, I knew I needed to be healthier in my cardiovascular system and not just my biceps and chest.

At the age of 50, while teaching my company's sales organization a seminar on goal-setting and how they could develop a plan of action to support their goals, I went way out on a limb and said that in order to show that these principles of vision and goal setting work, I would use them personally. Within one year, I would race a short, 15 mile triathlon. This was a really big scary goal, because at the time, while I could bench press a small car, I couldn't go up my driveway to the mailbox without being out of breath. I did not own a bicycle, and while I could swim barely enough to save myself, swimming a mere 25 yards would leave me out of breath and exhausted.

So, just like I described in the earlier chapter of this book, I wrote a vision with goals and a plan, and I began to execute that plan. I had to start slowly with walking, because my body was so heavy at 255 pounds, I knew that extensive running would damage my joints, and each day I would try to swim a little farther in the lake where we lived to reach my goal for the week. I bought a bicycle and I remember well the satisfaction that I felt that first day when I rode it 5 miles. On that ride, while I had a vision for doing a short triathlon, I really never dreamed that I would spend my Saturdays doing 100 mile bike rides through the South Carolina countryside training for the Ironman Triathlon.

Nonetheless, I persevered, learning to swim, watching my calorie intake, bicycling, and eventually running, and then the spring of the following year, I showed up at Parris Island, Marine Corps training base in South Carolina to race my first triathlon. It was a short "sprint distance" triathlon with only a 500 yard swim, a 10 mile bike ride, and a 6 mile run, but I completed it at my new weight of 225 pounds—still 45 pounds too heavy!

The jubilation I felt upon the completion of that goal fueled me to continue training and make a lifestyle of endurance fitness, and that year, I went on to race several more triathlons. The next year I raced longer distances, leading up to the decision to race a half Ironman, which is a total distance of 70.3 miles. As I built new health habits, my success fueled my vision and gave me confidence in what I was capable of, so I made the really *scary* decision to train for and race a full 140.6-mile Ironman triathlon the following year. The full Ironman triathlon begins with an open water ocean swim of 2.4 miles, followed by a 112-mile bicycle ride, topped off with a 26.2 mile marathon. It must be completed in under 17 hours.

I followed a 38 week training program, and during that time, I studied, experimented and learned so much about nutrition and fitness and what my body was capable of doing. I set my vision of seeing myself cross the finish line and hearing the announcer say in the traditional way, "Lee Fogle, you are an Ironman!" I visualized this daily during the grueling daily 38 week training regimen. During which my body was transformed from the 225 pound overweight powerlifter to a lean, muscular 185 pounds.

The next year on September 22 of 2011, I stood on the shore of the Irish Sea in the beautiful old seaside town of Tenby, Wales and at the sound of the horn, along with 3000 other male and female competitors, I ran into the ocean that was whipped up with 35 mph winds and 6-foot waves. It was a demanding race, and my finish was not very impressive, because the bicycle course was so windy it took me eight hours to finish that portion. Based on my time I received a DQ which means disqualification based on time, and I was crestfallen as I packed my bicycle and flew back home alone to the USA.

Determined to succeed with a good finish time under the 17-hour cutoff, I made the decision to try again. Slightly more than a month later, on November 4, I stood on the shore of Pensacola, Beach, Florida, and I raced Ironman Florida where I finished with a time of 13 hours and nine minutes. It was one of the most exhilarating moments of my life as I crossed the finish line after a long day of racing nonstop, and saw the proud face of my wife of 31 years waiting on me.

The purpose of telling you about this is so that when I talk about fitness and exercise and nutrition to you, I am not speaking of things purely from a theoretical standpoint, nor from the standpoint of a person who was raised as or became an athlete. I came from working class parents, I never threw a baseball with my dad, I played Little League baseball but as a child I'd never been to an optometrist, and had vision problems that we didn't know about. I had maybe one hit out of four years of playing baseball. I played high school football in a very small school where, in order to make the team, you simply had to have a pulse—again, no athletic prowess was required, so I made the team.

Clearly despite my decision to become an endurance athlete at the age of 50, most of my life was very non-athletic. I am speaking from the standpoint of a man who had to completely transform my habits and lifestyle through a moderate, regular disciplined program of increasing exercise. I studied and learned volumes about fitness and VO2 max and how to train using the heart rate zones of aerobic threshold and anaerobic threshold. I learned the discipline and value of doing long Sunday morning runs of 18 miles in a fasting state, having not eaten since the previous evening at 6 PM. I learned why over-breathing that results from mouth breathing while running interval sprints would create severe headaches and defeat my fitness goals.

Fitness became a lifestyle for the decade of my 50s. That was, until I got Covid in 2020, which shut down the pools and gyms and turned Tampa Florida into a ghost town. Rather than leaving my apartment on the 13th floor, I just stayed inside nursing my low energy, fatigue, and incessant coughing that later came to be diagnosed by my physician as long Covid. Despite knowing I had to "use it or lose it", I became a couch potato and I paid the price for that inactivity by the continual worsening of my condition. But I also turned that entire condition around once I resumed exercise.

I don't know whether you are coming from a life of exercise, fitness and good nutrition, or you're like 70% of Americans who are overweight. I do know that by starting slow and following a disciplined plan, you can put more life into your remaining years, and you can improve your life greatly. The key is disciplined exercise and good nutrition.

As with anything that I and others have done or may be recommended to you to do, start slow based upon where you are currently in your health and fitness. ***Be sure that your health will permit this and clear your exercise program with your regular physician, even if by simply calling and speaking to a nurse to inform them of your plan to begin a moderate exercise program.*** On that note, make sure that your physician is a *partner* in your recovery and will agree for you to report back to them on your results and progress. This improves the partnership and will also hold you accountable to your plan for improved fitness. It would be extremely rare for a physician to say that exercise is not good for you.

I typically do video/telemedicine visits with my physician for normal checkups, and the day before my appointment I email my physician the current status of my activities with a list of my health metrics including

- walking heart rate
- resting heart rate
- hours of sleep each night,
- amount and type of exercise,
- use of oxygen,
- any new symptoms,
- and general progress including energy and stamina.

She has never had a patient like me who took such an active role in their recovery, and she has expressed how important it is and how it is evident in my amazing health recovery results. She has been accustomed to patients who are very passive, waiting on her to fix them through writing a prescription.

Heart Rate and Heart Rate Variability as Measures of Health

The heart may not be one of the muscles you think about when you're working out, but just as other muscles in the body become stronger the more you work them, so does the heart.

Every time you exercise, your heart muscle becomes more efficient at pumping blood through the body, and it adapts to require fewer beats per minute to achieve the same level of blood flow to your legs, organs, and brain. When that happens, your resting heart rate, or how many times your heart beats per minute, lowers.

A lower heart rate — both at rest and during exercise — generally indicates a stronger and more efficient heart. Experts use it to measure cardiac fitness level. A lower resting heart rate also correlates with lower blood pressure, a lower body weight, and a lower risk for heart disease.

Runners use heart rate continually during most runs to determine how hard their bodies are working. It's important to keep in mind that heart rate can vary based on several factors, including:

- Age
- Genetics
- Gender
- Medication (beta blockers, for example, can slow heart rate down, while some thyroid medications can speed it up)
- Air temperature and humidity
- Stress or anxiety level

Numbers to know:

Although heart rate monitors come with any fitness tracker on the market, there are really only a few numbers you need to know to determine the strength of your heart, which you can easily calculate yourself.

These include resting heart rate, maximum heart rate, and target heart rate. H(heart rate is a good indicator of workout intensity because it measures how hard your body is working, not simply how fast you're going.)

RESTING HEART RATE

Your resting heart rate measures how many times your heart beats per minute (bpm) when you're calm and seated. The average resting heart rate is usually between 60 and 80 bpm, depending on age and other factors as noted above, but athletes can have resting heart rates as low as 30 to 40 bpm.

To get your resting heart rate, place your finger just below the thumb on the inside of your wrist or on either side of your neck and count your pulse for 30 seconds. Then, double it to get your beats per minute.

MAXIMUM HEART RATE

Your maximum heart rate (MHR) is considered the highest your heart rate /BPM should reach during exercise. It is very important that you know this maximum and track it because if you exercise at an intensity level above your MHR, it can be dangerous. I (it's why treadmills and other exercise machines have built in heart rate trackers and stickers warning you to stop exercising if you become short of breath or dizzy.)

To calculate your maximum heart rate, subtract your age from 220.

TARGET HEART RATE

Most experts and coaches recommend heart rate zone training, which tracks the intensity of your workout against your maximum heart rate and is expressed as a range of numbers that indicates how fast your heart should be beating during exercise.

Many athletes workout in a heart rate zone between 70 and 85 percent of their MHR. As an example, a 60-year-old man would have an MHR of 160 bpm and would have an exercise target heart rate of between 112 and 136 bpm.

Heart rate tracking during exercise can help ensure you're getting the most out of your workout but staying at a level that's safe for you — the middle ground between not pushing hard enough and overexerting.

Keys to heart rate training

1. Heart rate can be a great way to train if you want to measure your intensity. It can give you a ceiling to stay beneath on easy runs, a range to shoot for during workouts, and a warning if you're ever pushing at a dangerous level.
2. Also, paying attention to your resting heart rate over time can give you the satisfaction of seeing it drop — and your fitness level rise — as you put in the work, week after week. It may take a few months of consistent exercise for your resting heart rate to lower. It can take time for your heart to adapt to different intensities of stress on the cardiovascular system.

The lower my heart rate while sleeping, resting, or exercising, the ***stronger my heart is***. It simply means that my heart can pump more blood through my body without working as hard. I have carefully used heart rate as the measure of fitness and progress during my recovery from pulmonary fibrosis.

As an example, at my lowest point of poor health with pulmonary fibrosis while I was mostly sedentary and before I began an exercise program, I used 5 liters of supplemental oxygen continually and I could only walk short distances of less than 50 yards before needing to stop and rest. During those walks, my heart rate averaged 115 BPM. I was also quickly becoming hypoxic with oxygen saturation dropping to the mid-80s. My heart rate was rapidly increasing to supply the needed oxygen to my muscles, brain and other organs.

Over time as I walked a little farther each day, I observed my heart rate gradually decreasing.

After a year of continually increasing my exercise, walking longer, further and faster while also adding strength training and stationary bicycle training, my walking heart rate has decreased to 85 BPM without any oxygen supplementation. This means that my heart is able to supply enough oxygen to my muscles to do more work, and due to the improved strength of my heart, it can actually beat 30% fewer beats per minute to supply the needed oxygen. Clearly the oxygenation necessary for my muscles to function is sufficient. While measuring oxygen saturation continues to be important to me, my heart rate is more important, as it is available immediately moment to moment on my watch. The most widely recognized method for improving fitness and cardiovascular strength is to exercise, and the results of that show up as a lower heart rate. Be aware however that some medications including medical cannabis may lower heart rate artificially via the central nervous system. Confirm with your physician if any medications or supplements may be causing a lower heart rate.

About Heart rate variability

Heart rate variability (HRV) is how much our heart rate changes over time, and it can be used to understand how our bodies are recovering from stress throughout the day. **HRV is not only our most accurate measure of how recovered we are, it's also a measure of adaptability, our ability to respond to changes in our environment and bounce back from things that try to knock us down.** We all know it's harder to get back up after we've been knocked down and we're under-slept and overworked. An even more straightforward definition is that HRV is a gauge of our well-being. Pay extra close attention to HRV, because it is one of the most important health discoveries of the century.

Factors that *improve* HRV are:

- Quality sleep
- Slow, deep breathing
- Mindfulness
- Soothing touch
- Music
- Movement
- Nutrition,
- Gratitude
- Yoga and stretching

Factors that *negatively* affect HRV are:

- Stress
- Lack of sleep
- Unhealthy diet
- Alcohol consumption
- Lack of movement

No matter what the current level of your fitness is, *some exercise, even very light at first, will improve your condition.* I am certain of this universal fact that *not exercising and sitting on the couch most of your days will practically guarantee a deterioration of your illness and overall health.*

Use it or lose it. I had lost the Ironman conditioning over just 12 months of inactivity. In 2019, my exercise routines were a major part of my lifestyle. Daily, I swam 1000 meters at 7 AM, then ran high intensity interval training (HIIT) sprints with one of my dogs (while carrying the smaller dog) for 20-30 minutes— I walked and ran at least 15,000 steps every day. For errands and other appointments, rather than drive my car around downtown Tampa and search for parking, I simply biked everywhere that was under 10 miles round trip. Five days a week I lifted weights and used the stair climber in the gym.

That was all before COVID in January 2020, and the ensuing pneumonia and subsequent Pulmonary Fibrosis, which was followed by a year of feeling bad, fatigued, depressed and binge-watching TV while seated on the couch 15 hours a day.

But in December 2021, I had had enough of preparing to die! I knew there was still a full and impactful life I could live. I did a 180° turn and made up my mind that I would live a full and healthy life and be active for many more years. I vocally renounced the shortened life expectancy of 1 to 3 years remaining life that the medical experts had given me the year prior. It was brutally hard to change at first, but gradually, very slowly it began to get easier. Exercise is like the momentum of a flywheel; it may be difficult to start a heavy flywheel turning but each day that you exercise you give the flywheel a little push and soon the flywheel begins to create its own momentum.

My results in January 2023 after implementing a program of 52 weeks of consistent meditation, breath training, nutrition and exercise have been termed "miraculous" by physicians and healthcare practitioners and people who know me well—who saw me at my lowest point. But some "miracles" are just a result of hard persistent work—mine was.

First let's recap where I was in December 2021:

- I couldn't walk 20 steps even on oxygen without a two-minute rest.
- I paid dog walkers to walk my dogs twice a day.
- All groceries and food were delivered to me because I didn't have the strength to go out.
- Perhaps twice a week I would venture down the elevator and walk my dogs across the street. There was a slight incline going back into my building to the elevator and I can remember looking at it as if it were Mount Everest because I knew my heart rate would increase the moment, I started walking up that slight hill. I dreaded that hill that was only a ten-yard incline walk.
- In 2021 I was diagnosed twice with two different pulmonary embolisms due to my inactivity. It took about two months of proper nutrition, medication

and exercise to resolve those embolisms. They have not returned, primarily because I became highly active. The embolisms came as a direct result from my inactivity during the "*year of the couch.*"

- In December of 2021 I hired a personal trainer to help get me started and motivate me to exercise. She was a highly fit lady who looked like a model out of a fitness magazine, and I looked like a picture of a refugee from famine. It was absolutely embarrassing to have her help me down the stairs to our small gym in the apartments where I lived.

- I was such a wimp—she would have me do a few stretch cord exercises that exhausted me, she would then have me sit on the bicycle and pedal for two minutes which I could barely do. Lifting weights was out of the question, and I couldn't walk 20 steps without a rest.

- Total exercise time with my trainer was ten minutes in our small apartment gym, and the time to get me downstairs and back up to my apartment via the elevator was 20 minutes, after which I would be completely wiped out.

I accepted this challenge because I knew I wanted to live, and live with a good quality of life. While I might not be able to run marathons or do two-mile ocean swims any longer, I believed that I could reach a level of fitness that would allow me to participate in life, which I was not doing at that time.

Out of frustration I fired my personal trainer and to get started:

- I did exactly what I described in an earlier chapter in this book in terms of setting my mindset, writing down my vision of where I wanted to be long term and establishing my goals and an action plan to accomplish it.

- I initially set a goal of walking 5,000 steps each day and tracked it on my watch using the HeartWatch app.
- It took two months before I could consistently achieve 5,000 steps and it was grueling.
- Once I had achieved it I increased the goal to 7,000 steps.
- I then began an in-home Tai Chi routine and began to use stretch cords twice a day, and soon added pushups to my daily routine.

Gradually I began to see and feel results.

By April 2022 I was achieving 7,000 steps a day. In June I joined a well-equipped gym near my home. I have worked out in home gyms, small hotel gyms, and in my apartment with a stretch cord, but there's something motivating about going to a gym where there is lots of equipment, variety of exercises, and other people who are like-minded about their fitness. Since I'm in Florida, the first gym I went to had quite a few older folks in it, so I felt right at home with my oxygen tank. I am now a member of a large, busy, very high tech gym with a large variety of equipment and many people working out - young and old. But I am still the *only person I've ever seen in the gym wearing a backpack with an oxygen tank,* and it doesn't bother me at all. It's my badge of honor.

In May I began riding my bicycle five miles, two times per week, in July I began to play golf weekly and in September I took Pickleball lessons and began to play the fastest growing sport in the USA.

Below is a table comparing my exercise and fitness stats before and after implementing the program of exercise I have followed for 12 months.

Stats Before and after following a 12 month exercise program

Activity	Before	After	Notes/ Improvement
Daily Step Count	2000 **with** oxygen	10,000 **without** oxygen	500% increase
Steps/ minute	45	71	58% increase
Daily Exercise Minutes	5 min	70-90 min	In addition to time spent walking.
Walking HR	118 BPM	85 BPM	28% improvement
Resting Heart Rate (BPM)	80 BPM	52 BPM	35% improvement
Sleeping Heart Rate	75 BPM	52 BPM	31% improvement
6 min walk distance	320 meters	647 meters	102% improvement
SPO2@ Rest without oxygen	86%	95%	
SPO2 @ rest with oxygen	94%	98%	
SPO2@ under exertion with oxygen	84%	95%	
Oxygen flow at rest	5 LPM	None	
Oxygen flow walking	5 LPM	none	
Stationary bike on lowest setting heart rate	138 BPM	88 BPM	36% improvement

Before we begin your exercise program, you will need some tools for the journey. A good adage of management is that "you cannot manage what you can't measure", so you need to be able to track certain information to determine your current situation and measure your progress, as well as to alert you to problems on the journey of health. Consider your smartphone and your smartwatch to be your training partner and your accountability workout partner. Just as a good workout partner or trainer encourages you, affirms your progress and kicks you in the butt if you're not getting with the program, I find that a good fitness tracking app fills the same role, and it's practically free. The smartphone and the smartwatch cost money - consider them an investment in your life. I'll cover below how you can fund the cost of these items you need to track your progress.

Tools required:

1. Biometrics tracker—smartwatch: Top of the Line Apple=$300 Or Good quality other brands: $75-$180 Entry level: $50
2. Smartphone: $100-$800 but available with activation plan for $20 per month
3. Stretch cords: $20
4. Gym membership: $12 to $20 per month senior discounts available/ May be covered by your insurance
5. Total tools upfront cost low end: $270

How to afford them:

- Cost of a meal cooked at home $6. Daily cost $18. Eat one less meal per day for one month and you'll feel better and save $180. Two months = $360 = top of the line smartwatch tracker

- Forego eating out 3 times in a month @$20=$60
- Eliminate snack food: for two months=$80
- If you're a drinker of a glass of wine or a beer every day, stop and save $30 per week/ $120 per month plus feel better.

Total savings through healthy lifestyle changes: $620

Total tool cost: less than $300

Don't let cost stop you. It's an <u>investment</u> in your life and health that will pay huge dividends.

Where are you starting from?

- Review your health goals and vision from chapter three
- Refresh, refine or rewrite your vision of health
- Rate yourself as you are today on a scale of 1-10, in terms of achieving the health you desire?
- Record the following in your journal or in your computer

  o My current energy level 1-10
  o My current enthusiasm for life 1-10
  o My current belief that I can get better 1-10
  o My satisfaction and enjoyment of life 1-10
  o How many steps a day or minutes a day do I walk?
  o How many minutes per day do I exercise in addition to walking?
  o My resting heart rate?
  o My walking heart rate?
  o Use of oxygen while walking in liter flow?

- o   Use of oxygen while at rest in liter flow?
- o   SPO2 at rest with oxygen?
- o   SPO2 at rest without oxygen?
- o   How many meters can I walk in six minutes?
- o   Ride a stationary bike for two minutes on the lowest setting and record your heart rate? (Use oxygen if you are on supplemental oxygen)

Let's get you started with an example of the specific routine I've followed to recover from pulmonary fibrosis. ***Again, each person is different, and every situation is unique. Therefore, not all things will work for all people. However, my hope is that this information will help guide you and your healthcare team in determining which tools and techniques will work best for you and which ones won't be as helpful, or not helpful at all.***

My daily routine:

- Wake up at 6 AM
- Coffee without sugar at 6:30 AM. Note that I have not had anything to eat since the prior afternoon at 4 PM. We will cover the importance of not eating before bedtime and the value of a morning continued fast in the section on nutrition and fasting. A daily intermittent fast like I've just described is something I've been doing for about four years now. It gives me great mental clarity and focus in the mornings. I'm never hungry for food until about 11 AM, when I will break my fast for the day with a 2nd cup of coffee and a cup of unsweetened plain yogurt with walnuts, flax and Chia seeds. I don't eat again until midafternoon, which is my main meal of the day, after my gym

workout. I will eat about 4 o'clock and not eat anything else until the next day at 11AM

- Meditate at 7 AM for 20 minutes
- 12 minutes of
  - "4-7-15 breath training",
  - RRPF deep lung training (from Chapter 6),
  - Toe touches
  - Stretching using the T5T longevity routine (which is 1 explained at the end of this chapter). This routine improves my energy level immediately and helps me to be flexible and balanced throughout the day.

- Leash my dogs and embark on a two-mile walk. I call it my gratitude walk, and I turn it into a meditation each day. I practice breathing on the walk, I look for all the things that are perfect in the world, whether it's trees, sidewalks, manhole covers, houses, birds or all of nature. Often, I will listen to a book on Audible or a podcast during a portion of my walk. This walk takes about an hour since my dogs like to stop often and smell the roses, and then pee on them.
- Returning home, I will spend some time reading, writing, researching, or doing some work on one of the companies I have started.
- 11:00AM, I have a small, light meal of yogurt, walnuts, flaxseed and Chia.
- Next, I will do any sort of phone calls or meetings or handle administrative tasks.
- At about 2 PM I will arrive at the gym for an afternoon workout that consists of 30 minutes of hard strength training where I alternate days for upper body and lower body using the various

machines in the gym, dumbbells, or functional strength tools. I will follow this with 30 minutes of cardio training on the rowing machine, the stair stepper, or the bicycle. (*A very important part of this workout at the gym is monitoring my heart rate and increasing the pace or intensity to maintain at least 80% of my maximum heart rate, otherwise I am not effectively improving my cardiovascular fitness*).

- My goal is to workout at a pace that keeps my heart in the yellow zone on my Apple Watch heart rate tracker. The yellow zone builds fitness and is above 115 BPM, which is 80% of the maximum heart rate for a 65-year-old man. (**Max heart rate is normally calculated as 220 minus your age but confirm your own target heart rate with your physician**)

- I also strive to spend *at least ten minutes in the HIGH INTENSITY Red zone* of my heart rate, which is greater than 130 BPM. I wear supplemental oxygen in a C tank backpack while working out, and I will adjust the flow from 1 L to 5 L depending on the intensity of the exercise. I will undoubtedly go hypoxic (below 95% SPO2) several times during my workout, however for me I believe that is healthy for the mitochondria in my body during brief periods and it's something I have practiced even in my endurance racing before pulmonary fibrosis. It is often called high altitude or hypoxia training. Brief periods of hypoxia do not trouble me, and as I slow down my workout my SPO2 will return to normal in the 93 to 95 range.

On any given workout day, I will do multiple types of exercises in the gym. Some will be strength training, some will be high heart rate training zone work like sprints on the bicycle, or fast stair walking or fast walking on a treadmill incline. Each of these separate exercises may be only ten minutes per, and it gives me variety. Some days I'll just ride for 30 minutes on a stationary bike, doing intervals of full out maximum effort rapid pedaling for 30 seconds followed by slower pedaling to recover for two minutes, then repeating) Some days I'll ride my bike outdoors for 35 or 40 minutes, during which I will spend most of my time in the fitness-building yellow zone of the heart rate as shown below. ___Note: it is very important that as you begin strength training, unless you are already very familiar with weightlifting, or using the gym equipment, you ask the gym manager to give you a thorough orientation of a program of overall body, strength and conditioning that you can follow. This is a part of the service of any gym. They should also give you a written plan that you can follow for the type exercises to do as you build your fitness. All gyms will also provide an orientation to ensure that you are using proper form and levels of resistance to avoid injury.___

Here is a screenshot from my Fitness tracking app called Heartwatch. The screenshot shows the amount of time I spent in each of the target heart rate zones. In this workout I was doing high intensity interval training sets where I would pedal hard as fast as possible for 30 seconds and then slow back to a normal pace. This method "red lines" the heart rate, and then allows you to recover. High intensity interval training is a very well-known fitness science that you can read and study more about, but it's simple, and the principles work. I've used them for many, many years.

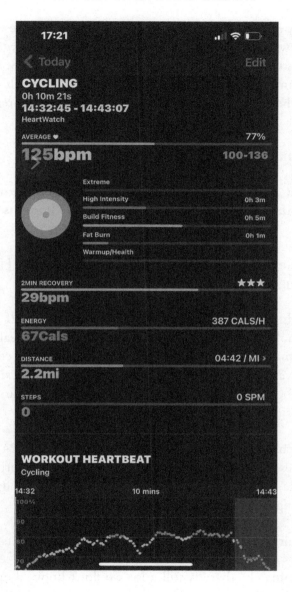

It is these high intensity, high heart rate workouts that have strengthened my heart and improved my fitness so that my heart doesn't work nearly as hard anymore to supply oxygen, and my muscles are stronger in and their ability to use oxygen. This is why I can walk four 4 miles per day without oxygen, due to the strength of my heart and cardiovascular system. As well as the improved lung function through proper breathing and strengthening the diaphragm for proper mechanical breathing.

Hypoxic training benefits:

If you are concerned about your oxygen saturation dropping during exercise here are some thoughts about that.

10 Benefits of High Altitude and Intermittent Hypoxic Training Michael Kummer

It might sound counterintuitive to deprive yourself of this vital molecule for the purpose of improving your health and performance, but as with other biohacks that seem counter-intuitive (e.g., fasting and cold plunges) acutely stressing your body by temporarily depriving it of its needs can have a net positive effect.

For example, depriving your body of food for 24 hours switches your body into fat-burning mode, kills opportunistic bacteria in your gut, triggers autophagy (the body's cell recycling and renewal program) and much more.

Intermittent hypoxia training also has several benefits.

Unfortunately, there is still a lot we don't know about how intermittent hypoxic exposure impacts the various organs and systems in your body. However, the research we do have looks promising, and my personal experience (based on the positive changes in my blood markers) has led me to incorporate exercising under low-oxygen conditions into my regular training and antiaging regimen.

The principal idea behind intermittent hypoxic training is that it can improve the function of your mitochondria, which are the parts of each cell that are responsible for converting food into energy.

From the foreword by Dr. Joseph Mercola in <u>Oxygen Advantage</u>, by Patrick Mckeon

> *"We all create a certain amount of free radicals through the very act of breathing, and incorporating breathing exercises designed to maintain a healthy breathing volume seems to be an effective strategy to keep your oxygen at an optimum level, and thus minimize free radical damage. Additionally, altitude training is a tactic many elite endurance athletes use to gain a competitive edge. One way of tapping into your body's natural resources is to purposefully expose yourself to reduced oxygen intake for a short period of time. This will improve your blood's oxygen-carrying capacity and also increases the maximum volume of oxygen that an athlete can use, known as your VO2 max. Of course, most of us live our lives close to sea level and do not achieve this benefit. But there are simple strategies that will allow you to access the benefits of living at a high altitude with reduced oxygen intake: keeping your mouth closed while you are breathing and practicing the various exercises outlined in this book. This is a challenge during intense exercise due to air hunger, but this is when most of the benefit actually occurs.*

An all-encompassing exercise to kick off your day:

T5T: The Five Tibetan Rites for Healthy Longevity

I came across this exercise in a book I was reading and decided to try it. After about a month I was hooked because I felt so great throughout my day, with even greater energy and stamina. I highly recommend it. Use the download and the information available on YouTube to start slowly and follow the recommended progression of this exercise. Start with only three repetitions of each of the five exercises. Every week add three more repetitions until you get to 21 repetitions of the five exercises. For me it's been life-changing on top of all the great things I'm already doing, this was the icing on the cake!

The Five Tibetan Rites for Healthy Longevity poster of exercises can be downloaded for free at https://t5t.com/5-tibetans-free-downloads/the-five-tibetans-poster-free-download, a copy is shown below.

The brief ten minute exercise routine energizes your body and mind in the mornings. You can learn more about it on YouTube at https://youtu.be/uEfEIsradMY

The benefits reported by many and testified to by me after two months daily use of the exercises are:

1. significant increase in energy - more the endurance type of energy as opposed to the revved-up caffeine type of energy. You feel like you can keep going and going.
2. Feel calmer and less stressed - your buttons simply don't get pushed as easily anymore.

3. Develop significant mental clarity with razor-sharp focus.
4. Feel stronger, more flexible, and less stiff. Enjoy seeing muscles appear on your arms, stomach, hips, legs, and back.
5. Good for toning flabby arms and tightening the abdomen.
6. Sleep better. Some people have more vivid dreams.
7. Overall improvement in your health, don't seem to catch colds, etc., as often.
8. Helps with depression and anxiety - lifts mood and improves well-being.
9. More centered and at peace.
10. Improved self-discipline and sense of purpose.
11. Feel younger and more powerful.
12. Improved breathing - deeper, slower, and more conscious.
13. Increased levels of Qi (chi, prana, life-energy).
14. Better posture.
15. Develops good core strength, which provides a strong foundation for any other form of exercise or modern living.
16. Some people lose weight; most find it easier to control weight and desire healthier foods. Improved digestion and elimination.

Source: T5T.com

Happy exercising folks! May you be blessed in your journey of recovery and may you see any obstacles as an opportunity to become stronger!

Chapter Takeaways:

1. Walk and exercise DAILY, make exercise and activity your lifestyle.
2. Do the RRPF three times daily which is for combined stretching and pulmonary rehabilitation.
3. Monitor your heart rate and see your heart become stronger through exercise!

CHAPTER 8

Sleep

By age 65, most of us will have spent 8000 of our 23,000 days of life sleeping, for a total of about 62,000 hours. A waste of time? Please don't consider sleep a waste of time, as sleep is vital to our overall health and longevity. We all know people who sleep very little who seem to be OK, and we all know folks who brag about only needing three or four hours of sleep a night as if it's a badge of honor, but long-term health studies have confirmed without a doubt that getting a proper amount of sleep and good quality sleep is vital to our overall health. Getting too little or too much sleep will have negative consequences on their health.

For a 65-year-old, the National Sleep Foundation (NSF) recommends 7 to 8 hours of total sleep every day. The NSF recommends against getting less than five hours, or more than nine, daily. According to consensus research by the American Academy of Sleep Medicine and the Sleep Research Society, sleeping less than seven hours a night on a regular basis is associated with adverse health including obesity, diabetes, hypertension, heart disease, stroke, depression, and an increased risk of early death. Less than seven hours a night of sleep impairs immune motion and performance in all areas of life, with increased errors in greater risk of accidents.

Total sleep time is important, but so is the quality, which is measured by the depth of sleep. Much research has been done using brainwave tracking devices and body movement to record the cycles of sleep. Today we have excellent true sleep tracking devices that will give us a tremendous amount of data about the quality of our sleep. This can enable us to fine-tune the factors associated with better quality sleep. Research shows that individuals enjoying deeper sleep are less likely to develop a cardiovascular risk factor for years to come. Additionally, since a person's ability to achieve deep sleep diminishes with age, poor sleep for one's age may indicate premature aging. I've gone through various phases of poor and good quality sleep. For many years as a weightlifter, I packed on protein and body weight. While I was strong, I was grossly overweight for my 6'1"frame, at 255 pounds. During those years, I snored and struggled with sleep apnea, purely because of being overweight and a mouth breather. I felt like I needed to get more air when I slept, so I used a neck roll pillow which allowed my head to tilt backward and open my airways for mouth breathing. That's the exact opposite of how we should sleep. During those years I struggled with dry mouth, sore throat, and continual sinus infections and conditions.

When I lost weight and became more physically fit, my sleep improved, but for years I continued to mouth breathe during sleep, which disrupted my sleep quality. There was a time during the high stress of being a global technology executive, working in global time zones which required conference calls at 2 AM, when I survived on five hours of sleep per day, but I paid a price. Leading up to my contracting coronavirus and the subsequent serious decline in my health and Covid pneumonia, my sleep habits were dismal. I would go to bed some nights at 10 because I was exhausted, and some nights I would stay up until 1 AM. There was no consistency in my sleep process. During those times I actually dreaded going to sleep, feeling as if I had so much to do I didn't have time for it. How wrong I was. I know that my quality of work, mood, and relationships suffered during those days.

If you are a mouth breather, or your children are mouth breathers, this will definitely degrade your health and your children's health. Again I strongly encourage you to read the book Jaws by Sandra Kahn and Paul Erhlich to understand how to become a nasal breather.

During a sleep study years ago, I was diagnosed with narcolepsy and sleep apnea. During that same time, I was also diagnosed with major depressive syndrome. It's interesting that depression, sleep apnea and narcolepsy all went away once I began to get a full night's sleep of 7 to 8 hours, and I began to a get full night's sleep *only after becoming a nasal breather*.

Here are some healthy tips to improve sleep:

- Use earplugs to mitigate potential sleep disturbances from a noisy environment, or if your bedroom partner is a snorer.
- Use mouth taping to promote proper nasal breathing while sleeping.
- Keep the bedroom cool, dark and as quiet as possible during sleep.
- If you have an alarm clock, especially one with a blue light, put a towel or something over to block the light.
- If you must go to the restroom at night and need a light, rather than turn on the bright lights of the

restroom, which will disrupt your sleep further, purchase a red night light that plugs into the outlet in your bathroom.

- If you cannot achieve a dark sleep environment, consider using an eye mask to block out the ambient light.
- Maintain a healthy body weight since an overweight condition is associated with significantly less deep sleep.
- Consume less caffeine, especially after 12 PM. Caffeine has a half-life of five hours meaning that after five hours half of it is still in your system, and it has a quarter life of about 10 hours meaning that after 10 hours 1/4 of it is still in your system.
- Discontinue tobacco use.
- Discontinue alcohol use in the evenings, and preferably completely. Since I track my sleep time and each day, I can notice from the eight or so measures if I had poor sleep quality, I have determined that even a glass of wine midday disrupts my sleep.
- Eat your evening meal earlier rather than eating food close to bedtime. Our gastrointestinal system needs 3 to 4 hours for gastric emptying, so eating within 3-4 hours of bedtime means that your body is still churning away digesting food when you lie down. This is guaranteed to disrupt your sleep, especially the most important beginning phase.
- Increase your waking physical activity but do any sort of workouts earlier in the day and not close to bedtime.
- Maintain good sleep "hygiene", meaning you should have a ritual that prepares your mind and body for bedtime. ***Falling asleep in front of the TV is highly disruptive to quality sleep and health*** for a myriad of reasons.

- Do NOT stare at a computer or phone screen during the hour prior to sleep.
- If you are watching TV in the hour prior to sleep, get a pair of blue light blocking glasses to wear. The artificial light of computer screens and television causes our retina to tell our brain that it's daylight and it's time to wake up, which is the opposite of what we want.
- Never use your bedroom for watching TV or working. Make the bedroom your sacred place for sleep (or sex) only. Whenever I look in my bedroom each day it produces a feeling of comfort just seeing it, because it is associated with such good memories of many nights preparing for and sleeping soundly and pleasantly.
- Maintaining a sleep routine of going to bed at the same time each night will definitely improve the quality of sleep.
- Having a set routine prior to getting under the covers helps us to fall asleep faster and sleep more deeply. Rituals and routines are comforting and send signals to our vagus nerve that causes us to relax.
- Pee before you go to bed to minimize and prolong the time before you're awakened to go to the bathroom. It's normal to wake up once a night to urinate, but following simple guidelines can minimize that and can help you fall back asleep quickly afterwards.
- Avoid sleeping pills that knock you out. These disrupt your sleep rhythm and leave a residue in your brain when you awaken. Talk to your healthcare practitioner about natural sleep aids as an alternative. A few that I have found helpful are L tryptophan taken 30 minutes before bedtime, chamomile tea prior to bedtime, and magnesium. There is a magnesium product on the market called

Calm that you can stir into warm water and drink prior to bedtime for relaxing and deep sleep.

- Medical marijuana is used by many folks for sleep. However, I have found that marijuana ingested in any form causes mood swings, depression, anxiety, and significantly lowers the quality of my sleep.
- Avoid watching tense, violent TV or movies with high levels of action or fighting prior to bedtime. For example, there is a great movie out about the 13 soccer players, who were trapped in a flooded underground cave, and had to be rescued by divers who went underwater in the cave. For a person who has lingering claustrophobia and has experienced shortness of breath, the thought of being in an underground cave that was flooded by rainwater is nightmarish, and that's just something I will not watch any time before I go to bed. In fact, I still haven't watched that movie because I don't want to carry those thoughts into my sleep time. One night, prior to bed, I happened to see a notice on YouTube, which led me down the rabbit hole of famous boxing match knockouts. I slept miserably that night with overactive dreams about fighting.
- I have found that using blue blocker glasses and watching a YouTube video on painting to be very relaxing prior to bed. There are numerous YouTube channels that involve acrylic or watercolor painting with piano music which are very relaxing.
- Meditation prior to bedtime is always very helpful to me. Either Guided Meditation using an app on my phone, or just reading a page or two in the meditation book and having a 10-minute meditation prior to getting under the covers, always creates a sense of peace and well-being for me.

Sleep tracking devices:

I started using a sleep tracker on my Apple Watch about 2 1/2 years ago. The app I use is called SleepWatch. I've tried several, but really prefer the daily report of my sleep from this app. Here is an example of the actual report that comes with the app and can be downloaded free,

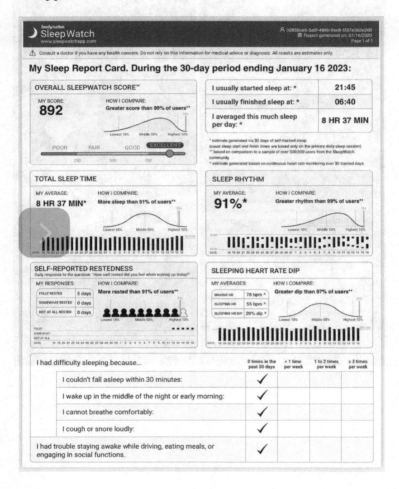

And here is the screen that I check each day upon awakening. The sleep score gives me immediate feedback on any changes in routine, diet, or other aspects prior to bedtime. Disruptions in my normal routine will definitely manifest in a low score with lower body metrics.

The following are my monthly sleep report graphs showing where my scores were in 2020 when I started using the app, and what they have climbed to by tracking my sleep and improving it through the feedback of the app. You can see how poor my sleep was, and how much it increased over time.

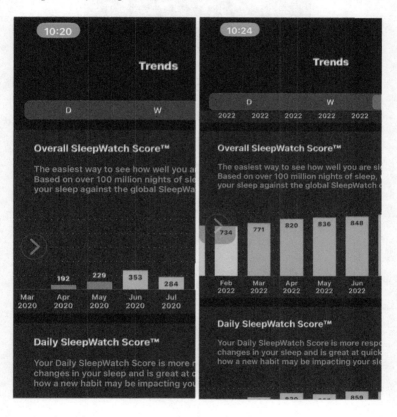

Through my use of SleepWatch over a 2.5 year period, my scores have improved 100% from where I started. I am now consistently in the 98th percentile of all users in my age group as shown below (this makes me giddy with excitement knowing how far I've come!):

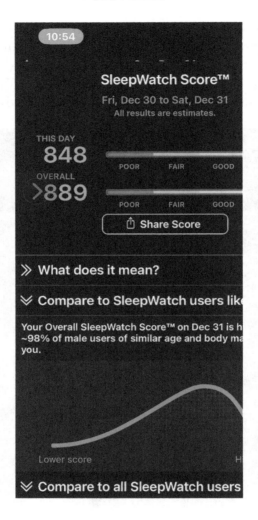

My experience and sleep protocol

In my own personal research to treat myself for lung disease, I have learned much from medical journals and studies and many health experts. But the knowledge gained from all my study was useless if I didn't apply it to my life. I'm a person who didn't always have a highly predictable schedule, in my life other than the ritual of waking up and meditating, which I began in my early 20s and continues through today. For as long as I can remember, waking up each day was my favorite time, and I began each day with a high level of excitement and enthusiasm for what lay ahead. However, in my earlier career two or three days a week, I was on an airplane, flying around the US or internationally, having dinners with clients or colleagues in different cities, and when at home dealing with household family things like bedtime stories or late-night help with a child's homework My bedtime schedule was completely haphazard.

Now that my children are adults and out on their own, and the coronavirus and the ensuing health issues I faced prevented me from traveling, my life has become more predictable. I enjoy that predictability and intentionally have created daily routines that give me a great sense of productivity, completion, contentment, and fulfillment.

My absolute favorite time of the day now is going to bed at night. I really look forward to the 8 o'clock hour, knowing that pretty soon I will start my bedtime ritual. This ritual is so comforting to me, it's become a sacred time. Recently, two very nice, attractive ladies in my neighborhood decided to pay me a surprise visit and popped into my home at about 8:15 one evening. As much as I enjoy their company, I immediately told them that it's too late for them to visit very long, and they would have to leave by 8:30 because that's my time to begin to prepare for bed, and I won't allow anything to disrupt it, even something as fun as being with them for the evening. Fortunately, they understood and have arranged subsequent visits earlier in the evening.

Here's my sleep routine that has given me so much additional health, peace, contentment, and enjoyment of life:

Pre 8:30 PM:

- I have eliminated alcohol completely (for the last 12 months)
- I eat my last meal of the day at about 4 PM.
- No additional snacks or dessert after 5 PM

8:45 PM:

- Brush teeth and wash face
- Take over-the-counter, all natural sleep supplements: L Tryptophan and Magnesium
- Let my pets outside for their last bathroom break

9:00 PM

- All lights in the home turned off except bedside lamp. Note, I avoid any sort of LED lights at night and use old style decorative low wattage incandescent bulbs in my lamps.
- Do 6 repetitions of 4-7-15 breathing (as described in the chapter on Breathing)
- Tape my lips to ensure I only breathe nasally while sleeping
- Read a couple pages in a meditation book
- Meditate for 10 minutes seated on my bed
- Stand up and do ten toe touches to stretch my back out before getting in the bed.
- Pee one last time whether I feel the need to or not.
- Get under the covers by 9:35 and turn on a sleep story from the Calm meditation app. (These are

simple bedtime stories on a variety of topics from traveling across Europe on the Orient Express to an excerpt from Gulliver's travels to describing all the stars in our galaxy that we are aware of. The sleep stories are read by men and women with great, soothing voices. Having used them for a year now, I can honestly say I have never heard the end of one, because I typically fall asleep within five minutes of starting a story).

- Reminder: *for best sleep quality limit any naps during the day to brief 20-minute naps prior to 4 PM. Also, only use your bed for nighttime sleep. Don't lounge in it during the day, and don't have a TV in your bedroom. Take a nap in your recliner and let your bedroom be a sacred place for deep and restful sleep.*

In summary, sleep is special, it's a sacred time to rest, rebuild and heal. Approach sleep with gratitude for this time that is yours for optimal recovery of health and life. I hope you wake up singing everyday as I do.

Chapter Takeaways:

1. Follow the guidelines in this chapter
2. Make bedtime your sacred special time
3. Sweet Dreams…

CHAPTER 9

Nutrition and Fasting

Assuming you have made a commitment to living a full, healthy and active life in your remaining years, and you have established a vision and goals and a plan to support that vision, and you have meditated on this and are instilling new habits in your life, and you have begun breath training, and are conscious of how you breathe and strengthening your diaphragmatic breathing muscles, *and* you have begun an exercise program, I'm sorry to say ***there is still something that can make your remaining years very difficult and end your life early.*** That something is the western diet also known as SAD, which stands for the Standard American Diet. Indeed, it is sad.

From age 20 to 65, I have been conscious of my health, I've taken herbs, supplements, vitamins, drank lots of water, fasted regularly, and eaten organic foods, but my diet was still poisoning me. My eating habits had been largely based around animal proteins and fats, with just enough vegetables and fruit to occasionally add some color to my plate. I ate chicken, beef, pork, or fish every meal. I actually felt I was bulletproof and would live well over 100 years. However, the threat of a drastically reduced life span of 3 to 5 years with pulmonary fibrosis, and the rapid decline of my health and stamina, I knew something needed to change. I followed my own prescription contained in this book of vision, goals, breath training and exercises, and the *last major change to my lifestyle* that capped off my miraculous recovery and healing was changing my diet.

The research I have done and the changes I have made have given me first hand proof. This portion of the book will lay out the science and reasoning and evidence for a predominantly plant-based whole food diet.

Vegetarians and vegans used to just frankly irritate me. I was a tough southern man who grew up eating rare steaks, fried fish and pork barbeque. I drove a 4wheel drive pickup truck, and I climbed trees in the South Carolina swamps to hunt deer and wild hogs with a bow. I personally butchered the animals I harvested, ate them and served them to my family. In addition, we ate steaks and chicken charcoaled on the grill almost nightly, cooked pigs on Fourth of July, drank milk by the gallon, and when traveling by car drove through Chick-fil-A for a 12 nugget special with waffle fries and sweet lemonade. Basically I ate all of the things that are the major contributors of the 15 top causes of death in America. I consoled myself with the fact that I took good vitamins and worked out regularly. But I did not understand that this common western diet is the major contributor to obesity, heart disease, cancer, high blood pressure and hypertension, Alzheimer's, and other diseases.

Bear in mind, I considered myself to have been a nutrition-conscious "health nut" for the last 42 years of my life. My children were raised on the evils of aspartame and high fructose corn syrup, white bread, and antibiotic-fed meats or farm-raised fish. They cringed when dad came in with a new idea for a new healthy organic approach to eating, as I threw out boxes of sugary cereal to be replaced by unsweetened granola. So it wasn't like I was ignorant about nutrition, I was very mindful and read much about proper nutrition, but I was just following the wrong path. I considered myself a Paleo eater, consuming the supposed diet of hunter gatherer cultures.

What I discovered in my battle to recover from pulmonary fibrosis is that I've been eating wrong! Terribly wrong. I was committing nutritional suicide In a way, and pulmonary fibrosis has literally saved my life. It interrupted my old eating habits and caused me to take a very close look at my nutrition intake, which will likely mean an even longer, fuller life than I would have had without it. It may end up extending my life because I changed my diet to remove the things that would truly kill me, with heart disease, stroke, or cancer.

People in their 40s, 50s, and 60s drop dead unexpectedly every day, and in most cases it is the food that they've been eating all their life that is a major contributor to their death. That could have easily been me, but pulmonary fibrosis took me up to the edge of the abyss. I decided that I wanted to live, happy, healthy, and active--not in a nursing home, on ventilators or a cabinet full of prescription medications.

In this chapter on nutrition, my greatest challenge is to condense the 1000 plus pages that I could provide about nutrition, food and fasting into 20 pages. *At the same time I feel a strong need to convince you that it is a great possibility that the food you're eating is contributing to and likely worsening your lung condition and overall health.*

Lung disease is the second leading cause of disease-related death. This can mean pulmonary fibrosis, COPD, or emphysema. Many of the signs and symptoms of COPD and IPF are similar, including **progressively worsening shortness of breath, chronic cough, tiredness, clubbed fingers, and weight loss**.

The information I used to personally convert to a new diet, a whole food plant-based diet, is gleaned from 20 different books, 50+ podcasts, and 100+ research papers that I've poured over, and have tested myself. The changes I've made have enabled me to recover my health and vitality from near and certain death. It turned out the same foods I thought were good and healthy for me would contribute to my death, whether from pulmonary fibrosis, or some other disease of aging. As a result, over the last 14 months, I have transformed what I eat. And I've never felt better, nor enjoyed eating and preparing my food more.

So, in spite of pulmonary fibrosis, my health and energy are at an all-time high, both mentally, physically and emotionally. The words that I'm writing to you are written from a strong healthy and happy heart. I fully believe the changes I've made to my own lifestyle will work for most people. As with much of the work on this book, I am writing this morning from a hospice house in Bradenton, Florida. ***Thankfully I am not a patient here***, but I am a volunteer on Sunday mornings, where I speak to the patients and the families who are arriving to visit their loved ones in the final stages of death.

Thanks to the nurses here, I get a list of the 12 to 14 dying patients that we have here each Sunday morning when I arrive. The list contains information about each patient, their diagnosis, their age, and their status. Often this list will be updated once or twice during my morning volunteer shift as patients pass away. One thing I always take note of as I look over the patient list is their ages—they range in age from their 40s to over 100, with most in their 70s.

I also note that at least 1/3 of the patients here are actively dying from a lung disease. This sort of shakes me, as I think back to just over a year ago. I treasure this reprieve that I have been afforded, so that I can accurately and carefully present factual medical, nutritional, and lifestyle information that can help you or your loved. Even though I have recovered so well from pulmonary fibrosis, I also know that there are many other ways that I could still meet an early death. I personally believe there is more work here on earth that I can do and more enjoyment of life that is ahead of me, so I'm doing all I can to ensure that I don't meet that untimely death.

There are many ways that you, the reader, can die early, but the causes are preventable with the information in the early chapters of this book, combined with this vital chapter on nutrition. In a published study on cardiovascular health, a group of long term marathon runners who ate a Paleo diet of meat and low carbs were compared with predominantly non-exercising, primarily sedentary inactive people who ate a vegan diet. When the objective blood markers of health for indications of high blood pressure, cardiovascular disease, diabetes, or cancer were examined, the couch potato vegans who didn't exercise *actually had better health markers than long term marathon runners!*

Certainly, I am not recommending you eat vegan and sit on the sofa for optimal health, but what this means is that if you followed all the instructions in this book so far, you could still kill yourself by eating a diet that is poisonous to your health. If you already have compromised lungs through lung disease, the last thing you need is cardiovascular disease, high blood pressure, liver disease, Alzheimer's, or kidney disease. We must have a strong base of health to strengthen our lungs, so it's important that we build strong immune systems and healthy organs to resist the diseases that often plague older people. *Most of those diseases are the buildup of a life of poor eating habits and or lack of exercise, and obesity.*

You may not like the idea of changing to a plant-based diet. I didn't like where my research led me. Food has always been a special way to enjoy life for me. Dining out in fine restaurants and steaks on the grill, were highlights of life. I still considered myself a very healthy eater because I ate grass fed beef, free range chicken and eggs, wild caught salmon and shrimp, and antibiotic free pork. I was very wrong.

For many years of my adult life, I followed a Paleo diet, which is supposed to be close to our ancestral diet. I ate animal protein at every meal, I ate enough chicken nuggets to fill a couple of large dumpsters, which would have been a better place to put them. I enjoyed eating I a large filet mignon cooked rare, hamburgers, grilled salmon, scallops, mussels, pork belly, bacon, pork tenderloin, etc. Meat was always my main course with something beside it such as a potato or starch. As I tried to eat healthier, I made sure that I had some sort of green vegetable beside my meat, but make no mistake, meat was always at the center of my diet.

After much research over the years of studying nutrition and practicing dietary changes but turning a blind eye to the harm that animal proteins and fats were causing me, I finally made the decision that a plant-based whole food diet would give me better health and longevity. The crisis point for me was the diagnosis of pulmonary fibrosis.

The beef, pork, poultry, and dairy industry take great exception to the research I followed, and in fact those industries have done all they could to squash the many research publications that prove beyond a doubt that an animal protein-based diet is very unhealthy and causes many illnesses, diseases and long-term health problems and early deaths. This knowledge caused me to change my diet and has made a world of difference in my mental and physical health. However, you must make your own decision.

Of all the research that I've studied, the best factual information about a life changing disease prevention diet is the whole food plant-based diet described in the book <u>How Not to Die</u> by Michael Greger, whose website NutritionFacts.org has a wealth of additional information. Rather than trying to recap everything in his book, if you need convincing beyond my personal testimony, I highly encourage you to read Dr. Greger's book. I have the Audible version and Kindle version, and it is my go-to manual for healthy eating. I also use Dr. Greger's app on my phone to check off my daily intake of the right kinds of foods.

What do doctors say?

Since research tells us that the Western diet is the number one cause of premature death and disability in the US, certainly it must be a high focus of medical school training, right? Wrong. Sadly, it's not even on the agenda for most schools. In a recent survey of medical schools only ¼ offer a single course in nutrition. And even though most people consider doctors to be very credible sources of nutrition information, six out of seven graduating doctors that were surveyed felt that as physicians they were inadequately trained to counsel patients about their diets.

As I asked previously, have you ever gone to a primary care physician or specialist who asked you to list everything you eat on a regular daily basis? Have they asked you about your daily activities? Have they counseled you on a detailed description of nutritional needs to fight and prevent illness? Probably never.

That seems to be the state of the medical industry, and to fix this situation, the California State legislature introduced a bill that would require physicians to get 12 hours of nutritional training at any time over the next four years. However, the California Medical Association strongly opposed the bill, as did other medical groups including the California Academy of Family Physicians. As a result, the bill was amended from this mandatory minimum of 12 hours down to 7 hours, and then reduced to zero. It's interesting that the California medical board has a main subject requirement: *a minimum of 12 hours on pain management and end of care for the terminally ill.* This is the sad state of modern medicine.

Thomas Edison predicted that the "doctor of the future will give no medicine but will instruct his patient in the care of the human frame and diet and in the cause and prevention of disease".

If we look at the number of pharmaceutical ads on television for various new "syndromes" being found by pharmaceutical companies, there's always a note to "ask your doctor about this or that drug". In studies of thousands of patient visits, the average length of time primary care doctors spend talking about a patient's nutrition is about 10 seconds if at all. The prevailing mindset seems to be to eat what we want, enjoy life and when we get sick take prescription drugs to solve the problem, we've caused ourselves through inactivity or diet or polluting our bodies with toxins.

Globally, over $1 trillion is spent on prescription drugs annually, and the United States accounts for 1/3 of that market. Most people assume that the diseases that attack us in older age are pre-programmed into our genes, things like high blood pressure by 55 years old, heart attacks at 60, and cancer at any time. However, the science shows that our genes account for only about 10 to 20% of the risk of most diseases.

The Mayo Clinic estimates 70% of Americans take at least one prescription drug. Despite this, we still aren't living much longer than others in the world. In terms of life expectancy, the United States is 27th out of 34 top free market democracies. And even though life expectancy has increased in recent years, the life we're living isn't necessarily healthy or vibrant. In 2011 there was an analysis by the Journal of Gerontology on mortality and morbidity. The question was, are Americans living longer now compared to generations ago, and the answer was yes, we are. The second question was, are those extra years necessarily healthy ones? And the answer is no. It's worse than that since we're actually living fewer healthy years now than we once did. *We live longer, but those longer years are lived sicker*.

When I visited my pulmonologist after the CT scan that showed my lungs were at an advanced stage of pulmonary fibrosis, he did not discuss my lifestyle or my diet, nor did he examine my method of breathing, nor recommend any immediate steps I could take other than supplemental oxygen. Our current healthcare model is a fee for service. Medical providers get paid for procedures and prescriptions, but not for results. Tufts Medical School provides the most education on nutrition physician training, which is about 21 hours, but that's less than 1% of the overall curriculum. In most situations, physicians do not get reimbursed for the time they spend counseling patients about the benefits of healthy eating.

Medical anthropologists identified the major areas of human disease, beginning with the age of pestilence and famine, which ended many years ago, and the stage right now, which is the age of degenerative and man-made diseases. We can see this in the changing causes of death over the last century. In 1900 the killers were infectious diseases - pneumonia, tuberculosis, and diarrheal diseases. **Now the killers are lifestyle diseases: heart disease, chronic lung disease, and cancer.** The emergence of these epidemic level problems of chronic disease coincided with dramatic shifts in dietary patterns. This can also be seen by what happened to disease rates among people in the developing world over the last few decades, as they have westernized their diet.

This epidemic of chronic disease is mostly the result of a near universal shift toward a diet of animal sourced and processed foods, in other words, meat, dairy eggs, or soda, sugar, and refined grains. China is an example of the impact on westernization of diet, since as they have transitioned away from the country's traditional plant-based diet, they saw a sharp spike in diet related diseases, such as obesity, diabetes, cardiovascular disease, and cancer.

The Center for Disease Control and Prevention (CDC), studied 8000 Americans aged 20 or older for about six years.

They found three lifestyle behaviors that had a tremendous impact on mortality:

1. People can substantially reduce the risk for early death by not smoking
2. Eating a healthier diet
3. Engaging in sufficient physical activity

The people who had at least one of those behaviors had a 40% lower risk of dying within that year. And those who hit two out of three cut their chances of dying by more than half, while those who hit three of the categories reduced their chances of dying by 82%.

Furthermore, the truth that has been shown time again through a myriad of studies is that four simple, healthy lifestyle factors will likely prevent chronic disease:

1. Not smoking
2. Not being obese
3. Getting a half hour of exercise a day
4. Eating healthier, which is defined as consuming more fruits, vegetables, and whole grains, and less meat

These four factors accounted for 78% of chronic disease risk. *If you manage to adhere to these, you may be able to wipe out or eliminate more than 90% of your chance of developing diabetes, 80% of your risk of having a heart attack, reducing your risk of having a stroke by 50%, and cutting your overall cancer risk more than 1/3.*

A plant-based diet in most cases may help prevent and in some cases even treat or reverse every single one of our

leading 15 leading causes of death including high blood pressure and heart disease, diabetes, and more.

Impact on health of a whole food plant-based diet:

If you have a dog, cat, or pet tiger, open their mouth and take a look at their teeth. Clearly their sharp pointed teeth are designed for ripping and tearing their food and not designed for chewing and grinding food. Now go outside to your barn, find your horse or your cow, or if you can catch a wild deer, they will do also. Now look in their mouths at their teeth. Not like a dog or a cat or a tiger, right? That's because they're herbivores, who chew and grind plants, while dogs and cats are carnivores. Now open your own mouth and look in the mirror at your teeth, notice any similarities with your tiger's or dog's teeth? None. What about your cow's teeth? Pretty similar huh? Our human teeth are more like a cow, horse or a deer. Classic herbivores.

As a regular meat eater, I never wanted to come to grips with this fact, but anthropologically, we were designed to chew and grind food, and the type of food that needs to be chewed and ground is plant based— fruit, grains, nuts, leaves, and stems.

What's robbing us of our life and health:

MORTALITY IN THE UNITED STATES Annual Deaths.

1. *Coronary heart disease 375,000*
2. *Lung diseases (lung cancer, COPD, and asthma) 296,000*
3. *Iatrogenic 225,000*

4. *Brain diseases (stroke and Alzheimer's) 214,000*
5. *Digestive cancers (colorectal, pancreatic, and esophageal) 106,000*
6. *Infections (respiratory and blood) 95,000*
7. *Diabetes 76,000*
8. *High blood pressure 65,000*
9. *Liver disease (cirrhosis and cancer) 60,000*
10. *Blood cancers (leukemia, lymphoma, and myeloma) 56,000*
11. *Kidney disease 47,000*
12. *Breast cancer 41,000*
13. *Suicide 41,000*
14. *Prostate cancer 28,000*
15. *Parkinson's disease 25,000*

Of course, there are many prescription medications for these conditions - statin drugs for cholesterol and lower heart attack risk, pills, and injections of insulin for diabetes, and blood pressure medication for hypertension. Medications are always isolated for the condition, such as liver, heart or kidney, but diet is a broad-based approach that addresses each of these killers. Dr. Gregor, in his groundbreaking book, summarizes from vast amounts of research and studies that there is **only one unifying diet that can help prevent arrest or even reverse each of these diseases.**

He states aptly that *"a heart healthy diet is a brain healthy diet is a lung healthy diet"*. The diet that helps prevent cancer is the same diet that may help prevent type two diabetes, as well as other causes of death in the top 15 list. The drugs which are targeted at very specific diseases also have a whole host of side effects and likely only treat the symptoms of the disease, while a healthy diet benefits all organ systems at once, the side effects are good, and most importantly, they treat the underlying cause of the disease. ***The one unifying diet that best prevents or treats these chronic diseases is a whole food plant-based diet.***

It's an eating pattern that encourages the consumption of unrefined plant foods and discourages meat, dairy products, eggs and processed foods.

This evidence-based diet and the vast amount of science that supports it indicates that the more whole plant food we eat the better off we are.

Face it, the majority of doctor visits are likely from lifestyle-based diseases, and that means that they are preventable diseases.

Physicians in today's disease management world of medicine are trained more on how to treat the consequences rather than the root cause of disease. They treat these by giving a lifetime supply of medications for risk factors like high blood pressure, blood sugar, and cholesterol. Dr. Greger equates this approach to *mopping up the floor around an overflowing sink instead of simply turning the faucet off.* Drug companies, big Pharma, are more than happy to sell you a new roll of paper towels every day for the rest of your life, while the water continues to gush from your sink.

*Dr. Walter Willett, the chair of nutrition at Harvard University's School of Public Health, said, "The inherent problem is that most pharmacologic strategies do not address the underlying causes of ill health in Western countries, which are **not** drug deficiencies."*

Kaiser Permanente, the largest managed-care organization in the country, published a nutritional update for physicians in their official medical journal. They notified the 15,000 physicians that **healthy eating may be** *"best achieved with a plant-based diet, which we define as a regimen that encourages whole, plant-based foods and discourages meats, dairy products, and eggs as well as all refined and processed foods. Too often, physicians ignore the potential benefits of good nutrition and quickly prescribe medications instead of giving patients a chance to correct their disease through healthy eating and active living.... Physicians should consider recommending a plant-based diet to all their patients, especially those with high blood pressure, diabetes, cardiovascular disease, or obesity. Physicians should give their patients a chance to first correct their disease themselves with plant-based nutrition"*.

Kaiser Permanente's proposed nutritional diet may work a little too well. If people begin eating plant-based diets while still taking medications, their blood pressure or blood sugar could drop so low that physicians may need to adjust medications or eliminate them altogether. Ironically, the "side effect" of the diet may be not having to take drugs anymore. The article ends with a familiar refrain: Further research is needed. In this case, though, "Further research is needed to find ways to make plant-based diets the new normal...."

Nutrition and Alzheimer's

Surviving pulmonary fibrosis only to be inflicted with the debilitating disease of Alzheimer's is not a happy future. There is very strong evidence that Alzheimer's and other diseases are also preventable with diet and exercise.

Autopsy studies have shown the loss of sirtuin activity is closely associated with the hallmarks of Alzheimer's disease which is evidenced by, the accumulation of plaques and tangles in the brain. Suppression of this is considered a central feature of Alzheimer's. The pharmaceutical industry is trying to come up with drugs to increase sirtuin activity, but the best approach is to just prevent its suppression in the first place.

This may be accomplished by reducing dietary exposure to advanced glycation end products, or AGEs. AGE are considered "gerontotoxins,", which means aging toxins (from the Greek geros, meaning "old age," as in "geriatric").

AGEs accelerate the aging process by cross-linking proteins together, causing tissue stiffness, oxidative stress, and inflammation. This process may have a significant role in cataract formation and macular degeneration in the eye, and damage to the bones, heart, kidneys, and liver. They likely also impact the brain, by accelerating the shrinkage of your brain as you age and suppressing your sirtuin defenses. Older adults who have high levels of AGEs in their blood or urine suffer accelerated loss of cognitive function over time. High levels of AGEs are also found in the brains of Alzheimer's victims.

From How Not to Die by Dr. Michael Greger

Where are these AGEs coming from? Some come from cigarette smoke, but major sources are "meat and meat-derived products" exposed to heat cooking methods that form AGEs. More than five hundred foods have been tested for AGE content, everything from Big Macs and Hot Pockets to coffee. **But meat, cheese, and highly processed foods had the highest AGE content**, and grains, beans, breads,

<u>vegetables, fruits, and milk had the least.</u> The top-twenty most AGE-contaminated products per serving tested were:

1. BBQ chicken
2. Bacon
3. Broiled hot dog
4. Roasted chicken thigh
5. Roasted chicken leg
6. Pan-fried steak
7. Oven-fried chicken breast
8. Deep-fried chicken breast
9. Stir-fried steak strips
10. McDonald's Chicken Selects breast strips
11. Pan-fried turkey burger
12. Oven-fried fish
13. McDonald's Chicken McNuggets
14. Broiled chicken
15. Pan-fried turkey burger
16. Baked chicken
17. Pan-fried turkey burger
18. Boiled hot dog
19. Broiled steak

Whenever fat is heated to frying temperatures, whether it is animal fat, such as lard, or plant fat, such as vegetable oil, toxic volatile chemicals with mutagenic properties (those able to cause genetic mutations) are released into the air. This happens even before the "smoke point" temperature is reached, so if you do fry at home, good ventilation in the kitchen may reduce lung cancer risk. Cancer risk may also depend on what's being fried. When meat is grilled, polycyclic aromatic hydrocarbons (PAHs) are also produced, one of the probable carcinogens in cigarette smoke. Air pollution studies suggest prenatal exposure to polycyclic aromatic hydrocarbons may then translate into adverse effects on children's future cognitive development (as manifested by a significantly lower IQ). Even just living next to a restaurant may pose a health hazard.

Scientists estimated the lifetime cancer risk among those residing near the exhaust outlets at Chinese restaurants, American restaurants, and barbecue joints. While exposure to fumes from all three types of restaurants resulted in exposure to unsafe levels of PAHs, the Chinese restaurants proved to be the worst. This is thought to be due to the amount of fish being cooked, as the fumes from pan-fried fish have been found to contain high levels of PAHs capable of damaging the DNA of human lung cells. Given the excess cancer risk, the researchers concluded that it wouldn't be safe to live near the exhaust of a Chinese restaurant for more than a day or two a month.

What about that enticing aroma of sizzling bacon? The fumes produced by frying bacon contain a class of carcinogens called nitrosamines. Although all meat may release potentially carcinogenic fumes, processed meat like bacon may be the worst: A UC-Davis study found that bacon fumes cause about four times more DNA mutations than the fumes from beef patties fried at similar temperatures."

Asthma and nutrition

From <u>How Not to Die</u> by Dr. Michael Greger

> "*Asthma is an inflammatory disease characterized by recurring attacks of narrowed, swollen airways, which causes shortness of*

breath, wheezing, and coughing. In the United States, twenty-five million people suffer from asthma, and seven million of them are children. A groundbreaking study recently demonstrated that the rates of asthma vary dramatically around the world. While such factors as air pollution and smoking rates may play a role, the most significant associations were not with what was going into their lungs but what was going into their stomachs.

Adolescents living in areas where more starchy foods, grains, vegetables, and nuts were consumed were significantly less likely to exhibit chronic symptoms of wheezing, allergic rhinoconjunctivitis, and allergic eczema. Children eating two or more servings of vegetables a day appear to have only half the odds of suffering from allergic asthma. In general, the prevalence of asthma and respiratory symptoms reportedly appears to be lower among populations eating more foods of plant origin. Foods of animal origin have been associated with increased asthma risk. A study of more than one hundred thousand adults in India found that those who consumed meat daily, or even occasionally, were significantly more likely to suffer from asthma than those who excluded meat and eggs from their diets altogether. Eggs (along with soda) have also been associated with asthma attacks in children, along with respiratory symptoms, such as wheezing, shortness of breath, and exercise-induced coughing. Removing eggs and dairy from the diet has been shown to improve asthmatic children's lung function in as few as eight weeks.

The mechanism by which diet affects airway inflammation may lie with the thin coating of fluid that forms the interface between your respiratory-tract lining and the outside air. Using the antioxidants obtained from the fruits and vegetables you eat, this fluid acts as your first line of defense against the free radicals that contribute to asthmatic airway hypersensitivity, contraction, and mucus production. Oxidation by-products can be measured in exhaled breath and are significantly lowered by shifting toward a more plant-based diet. So if asthmatics eat fewer fruits and vegetables, does their lung function decline? Researchers out of Australia tried removing fruits and vegetables from asthma patients' diets to see what would happen. Within two weeks, asthma symptoms grew significantly worse. Interestingly, the low-fruit, low-vegetable diet used in the study—a restriction to no more than one serving of fruit and two servings of vegetables per day—is typical of Western diets. In other words, the diet they used experimentally to impair people's lung function and worsen their asthma was effectively the standard American diet. Can asthma conditions be alleviated by adding fruits and vegetables? Researchers repeated the experiment, but this time increased fruit and vegetable consumption to seven servings a day. The simple act of adding a few more fruits and vegetables to their daily diet ended up successfully cutting the study subjects' exacerbation rate in half. That's the power of eating healthily. If it's the antioxidants, why not just take an antioxidant supplement? After all, popping a pill is easier than eating an apple. The reason is simple: supplements don't appear to work. Studies have repeatedly shown that antioxidant supplements have no beneficial effects on respiratory or allergic diseases, underscoring the importance of eating whole foods rather than trying to take isolated components or extracts in pill form. For example, the Harvard Nurses' Health Study, found that women who obtained high levels of vitamin E from a nut-rich diet appeared to have nearly half the risk of asthma of those who didn't, but those who took vitamin E supplements saw no benefit at all. Who do you think did better? A group of asthma patients who ate seven servings a day of fruits and vegetables, or a group who ate three servings plus fifteen "serving equivalents" in pill form? Sure enough, the pills didn't seem to help at all. Improvements in lung function and asthma control were evident only after subjects increased their actual fruit and vegetable intake, strongly suggesting that consuming whole foods is paramount. If adding a few daily servings of fruits and vegetables can have such a significant effect, what if asthma sufferers were put on a diet composed entirely of plant foods? Researchers in Sweden decided to test out a strictly plant-based diet on a group of severe asthmatics who weren't getting better despite the best medical therapies—thirty-five patients with long-established, physician-verified asthma, twenty of whom had been admitted to hospitals for acute attacks during the previous two years. One patient had received emergency intravenous infusions a total of twenty-three times, another reported he'd been hospitalized more than a hundred times, and one subject had even suffered a cardiac arrest after an attack and had to be revived and placed on a ventilator. These were some pretty serious cases.

Of the twenty-four patients who stuck with the plant-based diet, 70 percent improved after four months, and 90 percent improved within one year. And these were all people who had experienced no improvement in their conditions at all in the year prior to switching to a plant-based diet. Within just one year of eating healthier, all but two patients were able to drop their dose of asthma medication or get off their steroids and other drugs altogether. Objective measures like lung function and physical working capacity improved; meanwhile, subjectively, some patients said their improvement was so considerable that they felt like "they had a new life.""

COPD and Nutrition

"COPD Chronic obstructive pulmonary disease (COPD), such as emphysema and chronic bronchitis, is a condition that makes it difficult to breathe and gets worse and worse over time. In addition to shortness of breath, COPD can cause severe coughing, excess mucus production, wheezing, and chest tightness. The disease affects more than twenty-four million Americans. Smoking is far and away the leading cause of COPD, but other factors can contribute, such as prolonged exposure to air pollution. Unfortunately, there is no cure for COPD, but there is some good news: a healthy diet may help to prevent COPD and help keep it from getting worse. Data going back fifty years show that a high intake of fruits and vegetables is positively associated with good lung function.

Just one extra serving of fruit each day may translate into a 24 percent lower risk of dying from COPD. On the other hand, a twin pair of studies from Columbia and Harvard Universities found that consumption of cured meat—like bacon, bologna, ham, hot dogs, sausage, and salami—may increase the risk of COPD. It's thought to be due to the nitrite preservatives in meat, which may mimic the lung-damaging properties of the nitrite by-products of cigarette smoke. What if you already have the disease? Can the same foods that appear to help prevent COPD be used to treat it? We didn't know until a landmark study was published in 2010. More than a hundred COPD patients were randomized into two groups—half were instructed to boost their fruit and vegetable consumption, while the others remained on their normal diet. Over the next three years, the standard-diet subjects became progressively worse, as expected. In contrast, the disease progression was halted in the group consuming more fruits and veggies. Not only did their lung function not get worse, it actually improved a little. The researchers suggested this could be due to a combination of the antioxidant and anti-inflammatory effects of the fruits and vegetables, along with a potential reduction in the consumption of meat, which is thought to act as a pro-oxidant. Regardless of the mechanism, a diet with more whole plant foods may help both prevent and arrest the progression of this leading killer." Source How Not to Die by Dr. Michael Greger

Dr. Greger's simple stoplight system for what to eat and what not to eat for optimal health:

In his book and website is a simple system for identifying foods to avoid and foods to eat an abundance of. It's the stoplight method and is downloadable from his site NutritionFacts.org

Reprinted with Permission:

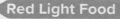

Red Light Food

Ultra-processed foods and processed animal foods. *E.g.*, cookies, chips, candy, soda, hot dogs, bacon, lunch meat, sausages, and oil.

Ideally, these foods should be avoided. Just like running red lights in the real world, you may be able to get away with it once in a while, but you wouldn't want to make a habit out of it.

Yellow Light Food

Processed plant foods and unprocessed animal foods. *E.g.*, bread, steak.

Ideally, Yellow Light foods should be minimized. The preferred role of Yellow Light foods is to maximize the intake of Green Light foods.

Green Light Food

Unprocessed plant foods—closest to how they come in nature. *E.g.*, whole grains, beans and legumes, nuts, seeds, fruits, vegetables, as well as herbs and spices.

Unprocessed plant foods tend to have more protective nutrients, whereas processed foods tend to have disease-promoting factors. For the Traffic Light System, think of "unprocessed" as nothing bad added, nothing good taken away.

NutritionFacts.org • *Evidence-Based Eating Guide* • **p. 9**

Red light foods: Ultra-processed foods and processed animal foods. E.g., cookies, chips, candy, soda, hot dogs, bacon, lunch meat, sausages, and oil. **_Ideally, these foods should be avoided_**. *Just like running red lights in the real world, you may be able to get away with it once in a while, but you wouldn't want to make a habit out of it.*

Yellow Light Food: Processed plant foods and unprocessed animal foods. E.g., bread, steak. Ideally, Yellow Light foods should be minimized. The preferred role of Yellow Light foods is to maximize the intake of Green Light foods.

Green Light Food Unprocessed plant foods—closest to how they come in nature. E.g., whole grains, beans and legumes, nuts, seeds, fruits, vegetables, as well as herbs and spices. Unprocessed plant foods tend to have more protective nutrients, whereas processed foods tend to have disease-promoting factors. For the Traffic Light System, think of "unprocessed" as nothing bad added, nothing good taken away.

Eat as many Green Light foods as you can, as little Yellow Light foods as you can, and ideally avoid Red Light foods, at least on a daily basis. Think of eating junk as eating for entertainment. You don't go on a roller coaster for transportation, but for amusement. Junk food can take your taste buds for a thrill ride too, but just like it would be unhealthy to live on a roller coaster all the time, it's unhealthful to live off of Red Light junk. Save it for a special occasion. The problem with all-or-nothing thinking is that it keeps people from even taking the first steps. If the thought of never having another pepperoni pizza turns into an excuse for not making the first steps towards eating healthy, focus on just scaling back on the pizza. It's really what we eat on a daily basis that has the greatest impact on our overall health. What you eat on special occasions is insignificant compared to what you eat day in and day out. Your body has a remarkable ability to recover from sporadic insults as long as you're not habitually poking it with a fork. So rather than thinking black and white or all-or-nothing, focus on crowding out less healthful options with more healthful, Green Light foods.

Beans: add to soups, chili, burritos, salads, and sauces. Blend with spices to make spreads for sandwiches or dips for vegetables. Puree beans with vegetables to make thick soups.

Berries: toss them into smoothies, oatmeal bowls, and salads. Cranberries and blueberries pair great with whole grain-based dishes, like a quinoa and kale salad.

Other Fruits: use in smoothies, salads, oatmeal bowls, or whole grain-based salads. Blend frozen bananas for a delicious Green Light version of ice cream. Bake apples with cinnamon.

Cruciferous Vegetables: toss into soups, salads, pasta dishes, and more! Red cabbage works well in tacos. Add broccoli and kale to your favorite pasta dish. Try roasted Brussels sprouts in your salads.

Greens: add to just about any meal or snack: smoothies, soups, stews, pasta dishes, and sandwiches. If two cups of raw kale is intimidating to you, chop it and cook it down.

Other Vegetables: use in soups, salads, stews, smoothies, sandwiches, and more! Dip bell peppers, carrot sticks, jicama, or cooked asparagus into guacamole or toss veggies into a smoothie.

Flaxseed: mix ground flax seeds in with oatmeal, smoothies, homemade salad dressings, or just sprinkle it on top of your meals.

Nuts and Seeds: use in oatmeal, salads, smoothies, and pasta dishes. Cashews, sunflower seeds, and tahini can be made into creamy dressings or sauces.

Herbs and Spices: Add ¼ tsp of turmeric to your smoothies, oatmeal, or any savory dish. Blend it with cashews, pitted dates, and water for an adventurous drink. Use it in curries and soups.

Whole Grains: mix up your morning routine with a bowl of buckwheat or quinoa. Add whole intact grains, such as barley, buckwheat, quinoa, farro, oat groats, or millet to soups and salads.

Beverages: the healthiest beverages are water, green tea, or an herbal tea called hibiscus.

Exercise: walking, running, biking, swimming, rowing, aerobics, dancing, martial arts, competitive sports, yoga. Find a safe activity you enjoy, and go do it!

As Dr. Greger cautions us, if the thought of never having another pepperoni pizza, or another steak, turns into an excuse for not taking the first step towards eating healthy, focus first on just scaling back the pizza and other yellow or red foods. It really is what we eat daily that has the greatest impact on our overall health. Special occasions, dinner out with friends, these are insignificant compared to what we eat day in and day out. Our body has the ability to recover from sporadic insults as long as we're not habitually poisoning it. I like Dr. Gregor's idea that rather than think black and white, all or nothing, simply focus on crowding out the less healthful options with more healthful green light foods.

My daily meals and supplements:

At one time a few years ago, I was taking probably 25 supplement pills on a daily basis and had been for years. It was a huge monthly expense, but each time I read an article about some way to defend against aging and age-related diseases, I fell for it and bought the latest, greatest supplement.

Two problems with that were that I never took any supplements away so they just kept adding up, however most of them were unnecessary if I just ate the right diet, which could provide all of the nutrition I needed. As I began changing my diet I slowly began to remove supplements without noticing any ill effect as I improved my nutrition with a plant-based diet. I am completely convinced that most supplements are useless wastes of money, and studies have shown that antioxidants and supplements just flat do not work to prevent diseases. Supplements cannot replace an optimal diet. Optimal diets reduce or eliminate the need for supplements.

With that said, there are a few supplements that are required even in a whole food plant-based diet due to the degradation of the soil where plants are grown, as well as differences in our lifestyle such as sun exposure. Based upon my research, here are some supplements that are needed in certain situations.

Vitamin B12 is not made by plants but is made by microbes that blanket the earth. However the chlorine in the water kills off bacteria/ microbes. We don't get much B12 in our water source as a result, so it's a good thing to supplement. I take 1000 mcg of Vitamin B12 daily.

We were evolved to make our own vitamin D from sun exposure. But most of us don't get enough sun exposure to make enough vitamin D, based upon an indoor lifestyle or being in a latitude where we get less sun. Therefore, vitamin D is something I supplement daily.

For lung health and greater oxygen uptake efficiency I take two things daily that I have noticed a huge difference from:

1. Cordyceps mushrooms are an ancient Chinese remedy for lung health which I've taken for 18 months. The actual mushroom can be quite expensive, but I take a 100% organic powdered mushroom that I purchased on Amazon for a very reasonable price. It only takes a small scoop daily to recognize a significant difference in breathing and oxygenation.

2. Beets are a super food for oxygen enhancement during activity. In a study on beets: n*itrates, concentrated in green, leafy vegetables, and beets, not only help deliver oxygenated blood to your muscles by helping dilate your arteries, but also enable your body to extract more energy from that oxygen—something never thought possible. For example, one little shot of beet juice has been found to allow free divers to hold their breath for a half minute longer than usual. After sipping beet juice, cyclists were able to perform at the same level of intensity while consuming 19 percent less oxygen than the placebo group. Then, when they ramped up their bike resistance for an intense bout of what they called "severe cycling," the time to exhaustion was extended from 9:43 minutes to 11:15 minutes. The beet-juice-drinking group exhibited greater endurance while using less oxygen. In short, the beet juice made the bikers' bodies' energy production significantly more efficient. No drug, steroid, supplement, or intervention*

had ever before been shown to do what beet juice could do. This effect works with whole beets too. In another study, men and women eating one and a half cups of baked beets seventy-five minutes before running a 5K race improved their running performance while maintaining the same heart rate and even reported less exertion. Faster time with less effort? To maximize athletic performance, the ideal dose and timing appears to be a half cup of beet juice (or three three-inch beets) two to three hours before a competition. I wish I had known that back in the days of racing the 140 mile Ironman triathlon!

3. To prevent inflammation and improve blood pressure I also add the spice Turmeric to my food daily.

4. To reduce my LDL cholesterol (the bad one) I eat five Brazil nuts weekly. They have an amazing ability to reduce LDL and keep it low for days. Too many is not good, hence my rationing.

Fasting

Before you run away screaming that you're not going to do long extended fasts, that's not my recommendation at all. Mine is more of a lifestyle of fewer meals, with more extended daily periods of not eating. For thousands of years humans survived on one meal per day, and sometimes one meal every two days. It is simply not true that we need three meals per day to survive. Three large meals per day plus the types of food we eat are a major contributing factor to the obesity epidemic in America today.

According to a multitude of studies on calorie restriction and intermittent fasting (or also known as time restricted eating) the health benefits are numerous. These methods have shown much promise in fighting cancer, diabetes, and improving cardiovascular health. Simply reducing calorie intake by 25% — not exactly a stretch goal given how Westerners overeat these days — slowed the pace of biological aging among healthy adults by 2% to 3%, representing a 10% to 15% reduction in mortality risk.

About three years ago, I began daily intermittent fasting as a way to improve my health and reduce my body fat content. I basically eat one meal per day in the midafternoon, with a small healthy snack (breaking of the fast) late morning before my daily workout.

Intermittent fasting worked very well for me and became a lifestyle. When I started, my weight was about 210 pounds, which was about 40 pounds overweight, and after a year of intermittent fasting my weight was 180 with a body fat percentage around 11%.

Here's what is meant by intermittent fasting:

Each day is 24 hours, of which about eight hours are sleeping —hopefully you don't wake up in the middle of the night and go down to the refrigerator to eat ice cream like they show on TV so often… Assuming you eat your last meal around 4 or 5 PM, then when you wake up in the morning at 7 AM you will have already fasted 14 hours. With intermittent fasting, what we do is simply extend that 14 hours long enough to ensure that our bodies begin the process of ketogenesis as well as another vital process for health called autophagy.

Ketogenesis begins when our bodies have depleted all the sugar/carbs or glycogen from our liver, which takes about

12-14 hours, and the body turns to its preferred fuel source, which is fat.

As the body begins to break down its storage of fat and use it for energy, our brains come alive with this preferred fuel source. To me that's the most exciting part about intermittent fasting - the feeling of mental clarity and well-being that comes with ketogenesis. Colors are clearer, vision is sharper, and I think more clearly and creatively. These are common "side effects" of intermittent fasting— amazing clarity and energy. And the very moment that I ingest sugar or a carb that clarity quickly goes away, and with a heavy meal or snack of simple carbohydrates and sugars, that feeling of clarity turns into a feeling of lethargy known as the sugar crash.

This is why the first meal of my day is between 11AM and noon. By then I have been without food for 19 hours, which causes my body to kick in another process called autophagy. That's a process our body uses to clean up our older senescent or dead cells. Our body literally eats these cells that are no longer serving a purpose, thereby recycling the various components of the cell, and discarding the toxins. The combination of these two processes of ketogenesis and autophagy are extremely healthful and invigorating and have become a way of life for me.

Often people speak of types of intermittent fasts in terms of the portion of a 24-hour day when they don't eat. For example, my day is a 19/5 fast, which simply means that I fast about 19 hours daily and then I have an eating window of about five hours where I do all my nutritional intake. There's no snacking outside of that five-hour window. It's also highly economical because I only have one major meal per day, since my first meal at 11 AM is just a small amount of plain oat milk yogurt mixed with Chia seeds, flaxseed and walnuts and a spoonful of organic maple syrup. For me, this is the perfect breakfast and sustains me through my workout at the gym in the early afternoon, after which I come home and cook an amazing meal that is whole food plant based.

I won't fill the final chapter of this book with all the recipes for delicious vegetarian dishes, but Dr. Greger's website has many great recipes. Just Google "whole food plant-based recipes" and you'll get tons of delicious, simple ways to prepare food for life and health. Also, a note, I do enjoy my cup of coffee in the early morning before I do my 2 mile walk with my dogs, so I have that cup, **without** sugar or cream, around 7 AM. This does not disrupt the above-described intermittent fast processes.

I firmly believe the combination of intermittent fasting and a change to a whole food plant-based diet has super charged my recovery from pulmonary fibrosis and given me the ability to live most of my life without supplemental oxygen. This has allowed me to be active in my community, both recreationally and by giving back through volunteer activities. This may sound crazy, but *life is actually better than it was before pulmonary fibrosis.*

Additional information reprinted with permission

 Beans: add to soups, chili, burritos, salads, and sauces. Blend with spices to make spreads for sandwiches or dips for vegetables. Puree beans with vegetables to make thick soups.

 Berries: toss them into smoothies, oatmeal bowls, and salads. Cranberries and blueberries pair great with whole grain-based dishes, like a quinoa and kale salad.

 Other Fruits: use in smoothies, salads, oatmeal bowls, or whole grain-based salads. Blend frozen bananas for a delicious Green Light version of ice cream. Bake apples with cinnamon.

 Cruciferous Vegetables: toss into soups, salads, pasta dishes, and more! Red cabbage works well in tacos. Add broccoli and kale to your favorite pasta dish. Try roasted Brussels sprouts in your salads. [10]

 Greens: add to just about any meal or snack: smoothies, soups, stews, pasta dishes, and sandwiches. If two cups of raw kale is intimidating to you, chop it and cook it down.

 Other Vegetables: use in soups, salads, stews, smoothies, sandwiches, and more! Dip bell peppers, carrot sticks, jicama, or cooked asparagus into guacamole or toss veggies into a smoothie.

 Flaxseed: mix ground flax seeds in with oatmeal, smoothies, homemade salad dressings, or just sprinkle it on top of your meals.

 Nuts and Seeds: use in oatmeal, salads, smoothies, and pasta dishes. Cashews, sunflower seeds, and tahini can be made

Here are excerpts from Dr. Greger's NutritionFacts.org, which has a free downloadable pdf with these helpful guides pictured below.

Simply following these including the Red, Yellow, Green Light will make changing your nutrition simple and easier.

In closing, people are wearing anti Covid masks while walking their dog alone and then eating highly processed junk food that has a 60% chance of killing them while CoVid has a .035% chance of killing them. They're sending their kids to school with a mask and hand sanitizer, but they ate Fruit Loops and milk for breakfast.

There was a time during endurance training when I viewed food simply as fuel, but most of my life I viewed fine dining as a great pleasure of life. Today I view food as medicine– but medicine that also serves the purpose of fuel and that can be pleasurable to cook and enjoy.

Happy dining!

Chapter Takeaways

1. For optimal health and longevity, a mostly plant-based diet is key.
2. The internet is filled with great ways to prepare a plant-based diet. (Google Ikarian Longevity Stew and try out this amazing meal from the Blue Zones).
3. A reduced calorie diet with regular periods of fasting has been shown in numerous studies to promote long healthy aging and disease fighting characteristics.

Chapter 10

Conclusion

From today's news headlines:

Millionaire Spends Over $2 Million In An Attempt To Make His Body Young Again Multi-millionaire Bryan Johnson has spent over $2 million in an attempt to de-age himself. The 45-year-old hired a team of medical professionals to help him, according to Bloomberg, "have the brain, heart, lungs, liver, kidneys, tendons, teeth, skin, hair, bladder, penis, and rectum of an 18-year-old". So far Johnson's team has focused on the unsurprising: developing a diet and exercise regimen. If you eat and drink right and get regular exercise you will improve your overall fitness, probably more so when you've spent large sums on a team to help you stick to it. Johnson sticks to a 1,977-calorie vegan diet, and even sticks to a sleep schedule.

Hmmm… $2 million? And his medical specialists are basically recommending the methods in this book. Did I underprice the book? No. I think he's overpaying for his advice and plan.

A long and healthy life is largely a matter of choice. One religious scripture I have always held a firm belief in is from the book of Deuteronomy 30:19, which reads *"I have set before you life and death, blessing and curse. Therefore, choose life that you and your offspring may live."*

We are called to CHOOSE life. Choosing life means all the minute decisions we make hundreds of times a day—whether to buckle our seat belt, eat three donuts or carrots instead, stay up until midnight watching street fights on YouTube or meditate and go to bed at 9:30. Drink a couple beers with friends and then drive to the store, criticize others, complain about our job or health, or dwell on positive things in our life and the world around us…choices of life or death. I hope that this story of my personal journey demonstrates the choices I've made that have set my own feet on a path of a full, active, and restored life, and that you can see these same choices may help you in recovering from lung disease.

Understanding and believing that the quality of our lives is our choice gives us a level of personal responsibility for our life. We're not just blown here and there by the whims of some mysterious capricious fate, but we are the captain of our own destiny. Wherever I am right now, I am responsible for putting myself here.

The people who survive horrible illnesses, diseases, and accidents, or live with severe handicaps and still persevere are people who believe that. We are the people who look for the opportunity in any calamity or circumstance to pull through, overcome, rise above, and be strong in the face of adversity. There's a great book I read by Ryan Holiday called The Obstacle is the Way, and I have seen that truth often in my life where the obstacles that I encountered opened the door to new opportunities or a new way to live, and I emerged stronger with a better appreciation for life with more gratitude and more wisdom.

Loneliness

Loneliness sucks. Loneliness has more than a twofold effect on mortality than obesity. Here at the hospice house this Sunday morning, I noted that two of the 12 dying people have large families coming and going to be with them. But 10 of the patients in the final stages of dying have no one visiting. On any given day here at the hospice house, I see a similar trend. Only about 20% of the patients have visitors on Sundays. But it's not like these people will be here for weeks or months and people can visit them anytime. When they enter hospice, they likely have only a few days of life left. Sadly, no one visits over half of these folks, and so we, the staff and volunteers, are the only faces they see in their final hours.

I've been in a place with no family or friends. I had a full life raising three children to adulthood in a close community and large church. I had a job where I knew thousands of people and had many friendships. My wife and I had been married for 31 years, but upon becoming empty nesters we decided to divorce. Our children took it hard, and our community took sides. My life, which had been built upon the core of family, was quickly shattered into many pieces. After that I moved from my lifetime home in South Carolina across the country to San Francisco, where I knew no one. Subsequently I have lived in several cities; San Francisco, Tampa, Sarasota, all alone with very few friends nearby. Today my former wife and I are still friends, but she lives in South Carolina, as do two of my adult children, and so my opportunities to see them have been very rare.

The year that I suffered from long Covid pneumonia, and the resulting pulmonary fibrosis was one of the loneliest times of my life. I really had no one. The condos and apartments I'd lived in were great hook-up spots for people 20 to 30 years younger than me— transient tenets with whom I had little in common. I knew that isolation was not good for my health, so I followed my own prescription discussed earlier in this book, and I cast a new vision with my intention to become socially engaged with the world around me. That led me to move to Bradenton, FL, to a 55+ retirement community where I could get to know others my age.

I'm happy to say it has worked wonderfully. I'm a part of a very active community of people who invite each other over, hold community events, and are just really good neighbors. Just walking around my neighborhood has done more for my social life than anything. My evening walks are peppered with conversations with neighbors that I've learned to treasure. I stroll with my dogs and talk to people out in their yards every evening. The walk doesn't have to be a heads-down mission to cover as much ground in the shortest time as possible. I prefer strolling and pausing to talk to neighbors, which turns my 20 minute evening walk into an hour--a social hour.

This is adapted from Robert Waldinger and Marc Schulz's new book, The Good Life: Lessons From the World's Longest Scientific Study of Happiness.

According to The Good Life, Loneliness has a physical effect on the body. It can render people more sensitive to pain, suppress their immune system, diminish brain function, and disrupt sleep, which in turn can make an already lonely person even more tired and irritable. Research has found that, for older adults, loneliness is far more dangerous than *obesity. Ongoing loneliness raises a person's odds of death by <u>26 percent</u> in any given year. A study in the U.K., the Environmental Risk (E-Risk) Longitudinal Twin Study, <u>recently reported</u> on the connections between loneliness and poorer health and self-care in young adults. This ongoing study includes more than 2,200 people born in England and Wales in 1994 and 1995. When they were 18, the researchers asked them how lonely they were. Those who reported being lonelier had a greater chance of facing mental-health issues, partaking in unsafe physical-health behaviors, and coping with stress in negative ways. Add to this the fact that a tide of loneliness is flooding through modern societies, and we have a serious problem. Recent stats should make us take notice.*

<u>The six protective factors in aging</u> *also from the longest longitudinal study on aging and the book <u>Aging Well</u> by George E. Vaillant, MD*

AGING WELL: SURPRISING GUIDEPOSTS TO A HAPPIER...

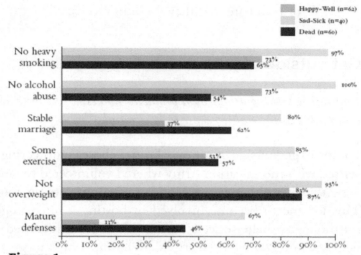

Figure 1

Predictor Values at Age 50 of Successful Aging of Harvard Sample at Age 75–80

Four Personal Qualities for aging well:

1. The first quality is future orientation, the ability to anticipate, to plan and to hope.
2. The second quality is a capacity for gratitude and forgiveness, the capacity to see the glass of life as half-full, not half-empty. Put differently, Thanksgiving is not "just another day" and paranoia and injustice-collecting can destroy old age.
3. The third quality is being able to imagine the world as it seems to the other person, the capacity to love and to hold the other empathically—but loosely.

4. The fourth quality, related to the third, is the desire to do things with people, not to do things to people or ruminate that they do things to us.

Get outside of your own head.

Constantly looking at our own problems makes us feel miserable and makes us miserable people to be around.

For me to get outside of my own head, I chose volunteering. I started with the Salvation Army where I volunteered to work with the men's shelter on Monday evenings serving food. This led me to become involved in hosting a bingo night for the men's shelter once a month. Next, I was recruited to help with the Young at Heart(elderly)group which meets on Wednesdays. The group provides a speaker and a program such as gardening or line dancing (which is led by a blind woman— what a great example of not nursing your problems or circumstances but giving to the world instead), a lunch, and a social avenue for about 20 to 30 elderly folks from the community. I saw it as an opportunity to pitch in and went from serving and cooking food for them to leading them in Thai Chi and limited exercise. This led me to develop a seminar on tips for healthy aging, which I have begun to provide to this group and others at no cost.

Not long ago based on my rapid decline I was considering moving to assisted-living and palliative care and subsequently to hospice. Once I became healthy enough to be a little more active I went through the training to become a volunteer for hospice. I learned a great deal through the process and now I am active in a weekly volunteer shift where I greet and talk to families and patients in our hospice house, as well as visiting and providing respite care for some of the elderly patients who are still in their home. I even get to spend time with centenarians occasionally. Last week, I was with a 101-year-old gentleman who is a delight to be around. I also spend time with Alzheimer's patients in the memory care center. These opportunities are moments I treasure, because I feel so much gratitude as I sit and talk with folks whose days are numbered, as all of our days are. Theirs are just much shorter.

Some "tough love' for Support groups

There are many Facebook support groups for pulmonary fibrosis. They provide an organized forum for exchanging information and asking and answering questions related to lung disease. I have been a member of several of these groups and a contributor to them in terms of comments and posts and answering questions. I also have been a member of two different zoom weekly support groups which are small 5 to 6 person closed groups that are by invitation only. These groups provide a consistent group of people from all over the country on Zoom that develop into a community of people sharing their journey with pulmonary fibrosis.

Here are some pros and cons on Facebook support groups:

Pros:

- A moderated forum for exchange of information.
- A forum to ask questions to get answers from people who may have had a similar experience.

- An opportunity to learn from one another, and each other's experiences with the disease of pulmonary fibrosis.
- The place for caregivers to talk to folks who have the disease other than their loved ones.
- A place for newcomers coming to grips with their diagnosis where lots of supporters are willing to help and encourage them.
- The Facebook groups are very strict about preventing advertisements or selling products.

Cons:

- There's not a lot of positive optimism in most of the groups I've been around.
- Many people share their concerns about their disease and appear to have little to no hope for life getting any better, And other than nice, kind, sympathetic platitudes of "keep your chin up", "you'll get through this" etc. it's really not a lot of clear, positive experience-based help for them.
- Group admins are extremely cautious and often quite hawkish about anyone giving recommendations, or describing even simple ideas about how natural herbs, exercise and nutrition have helped them.

I've had great results with my recovery, and any time I have posted about my progress, especially with respect to exercising regularly, I get hundreds of comments from people thanking me and stating that my progress gives them hope. However, _invariably_, my optimistic post comments will be cautiously admonished by the group moderator who takes it upon themself to point out to everyone that they should "_not_ *all expect to get similar results because we're not all at the same place in our illness, and before you do anything that others are doing you should check with your doctor, blah blah blah."*

It's as if some moderators have an innate desire to throw a wet blanket on anything resembling hope. And as far as the constant admonition to "check with your doctor" before starting to exercise, or even do breathing exercises, I find that ludicrous. I have spoken to countless people who have trouble getting a doctor's appointment. It takes weeks to get one, maybe months, and when they finally do, the doctor spends less than five minutes with them and answers almost none of their questions. People are paralyzed into inactivity over the simplest of things like just beginning a walking program. One thing I would say is that if your doctor tells you that you shouldn't be walking for exercise, you probably want to get a second opinion and maybe a different doctor.

I once posted an update on Facebook with a pulmonary support group describing how I previously couldn't walk 20 steps without assistance, but with daily exercise and nutrition I am now working out in the gym. And, like most Facebook posts, I put a video at the beginning that showed me in the gym with an oxygen tank in a backpack doing 24-inch box jumps. Within one hour 400 people had responded and commented positively about how the post had given them such hope. They were so excited to see what I was able to do even with pulmonary fibrosis in the advanced stages.

However, my post was removed because I had placed the video at the beginning of the post rather than put it in the comment section. I was also <u>warned</u> by the administrator that I would be banned from the group if I did that again. Surely the moderator must work for some bureaucratic arm of the US government where they put rules above everything. Amazing.

Recently, I was in a support group video conference for the well-known national IPF group. Their group calls are always excellent, informative, and well moderated. There was a nurse speaking to the group about the topic of "grief" in this meeting, and she asked for examples from the attendees about any personal grief that they felt in the loss of their health. There were several very sad shares from others, and during a lull in the comments, I responded and described how I previously felt intense grief over the degradation of my health, but how I had changed my lifestyle with nutrition and exercise, and now my life is positive and active. As I was describing how good my life is now, and the actual improvement in pulmonary function, the grief counselor interrupted me rudely and said thank you Lee, but let's stay on the topic of grief. *Can you believe that? Let's talk about grief, but let's not talk about how to emerge from grief to health and optimism for life. Unbelievable!*

Another example of the danger of optimism, I was recently asked to leave a support group I've been meeting with weekly for several months. There were about six of us in the group from around the country. It was not a very motivated group and consisted mainly of guys sitting around in their recliners talking about the weather and was mostly small talk, which they seemed happy with. Maybe I should've just left the group, but I always tried to bring something positive to the conversation. I typically described some new exercise or nutrition fact, or something else that I was doing and getting good results from. A few weeks ago, though, I was asked to leave the group because the moderator thought that I made others feel uncomfortable and "bad" because of the progress that I was making and they weren't. Hmmmm...Let's get a group of sick people together to discuss how sick we are and why we're not higher on the transplant list, but let's not discuss any life changes that might help us get well...

The good news is that I was asked to join a new group which consists of six people, three of whom are former nurses, and they all are enthusiastically looking at alternatives, and embracing the topic of overcoming the disease of IPF. They have great intellectual curiosity and quickly absorb new ideas and do their own research. Each time I interact with this group I come away, feeling truly supported.

While asking the opinions of a Facebook support group on how I should title this book, a lady expressed gratitude or the fact I was writing a book and she wanted to read it once it was published. She was immediately replied to by a person who disparaged the concept of my book and stated that it was deceptive because you cannot recover from IPF and the book would give false hope to people.

So just know that all support groups are not necessarily a place to get support and uplifting advice on getting better—shop around and find one that you can fit into. Some are a place with sadness and grief, but also lots of healthy compassion. It is, however, difficult to find much optimism and good, verified new health advice. It is difficult in those environments to restrain myself when I have found such renewed health and strength. I want to share it with the world, however, I try to dial that enthusiasm back and just answer peoples' questions with compassion and <u>my own personal experience</u> if it's relative. But I always issue the caveat that "*this is not medical advice, and I'm not a doctor blah blah blah.*"

Final thoughts

Be open minded in your search for ways of healthy living that can promote wellness. Do your own research, compile your questions before you go to your physician's appointment, and send them by email beforehand. Make sure the doctor gets them and be your own advocate. Research supposed cures, because there is a lot of snake oil out there, and many reports and research papers are funded by commercial entities or big Pharma, trying to sell you a new pill or some new herbal remedy.

Some new remedies may work, that's how we evolve healthcare. The FDA is not going to evolve healthcare, but physicians working hand in hand with patients being open to new ideas will develop treatments faster. I took the approach with my own recovery of a broad-based attack on the enemy, which was the illness, and I tried many things at once. I used exercise, low light laser therapy, cold therapy, breath training, a complete change in nutrition etc. I didn't wait on the doctor to make me well. If you're waiting on the FDA to approve a pill and cure you, you will likely die or get much worse before all the clinical trials are ever done.

Some readers may feel offended that I have been unfairly dismissive of pharmaceutical approaches and medications for pulmonary fibrosis. I don't intend to be dismissive, however, if your only strategy to prevent disease or recover from a disease is a medication, then it's likely not enough. Medications can be one component in the strategy for health, but the overall strategy must include nutrition, exercise, and a positive mindset to be most effective.

There is no single pill that is effective at stopping or reversing this disease, but the steps that I have outlined in this book I have taken personally, and they're working for me. They may not work for you, but what have you got to lose? At the end of this chapter, in the appendix, there is a list of 54 things I've tried. I've given them a rating of 0 to 5 stars and a little bit of a description. You may reach me at my email address leefogle1@gmail.com to ask questions about any of these.

Lastly, build your life around healthy activities and exercise, don't try to fit exercise into your life, build a day full of activity and fit the rest of your life into that day.

May you be blessed with longer life, stamina, endurance, and a healthy recovery and may you know a deep peace and joy in your heart.

Lee

APPENDIX

Tried	Helped Y/N	Effectiveness Rating 1L-5H	Comments
Whole food plant based diet	Y	★ ★ ★ ★ ★	Has taken my overall health and lung recovery to a new level. Feel great, stamina, mood, weight, etc.
Cordyceps mushrooms	Y	★ ★ ★ ★ ★	Improved breathing noticeably. I use it daily.
Low Dose Naltrexone 4.5 mg	Y	★ ★ ★ ★ ★	Reduced inflammation. Used in Long Covid protocols often. Promotes healthy levels of glutathione and protects cells from oxidative damage. Also has been shown to support immune response and respiratory function. Used for 12 months during recovery.
DAILY Strenuous Exercise	Y	★ ★ ★ ★ ★	Excellent results in every way.
Daily Walking for 1 to 2 hours	Y	★ ★ ★ ★ ★	Reduces early mortality rate by 24%.

O2 Trainer	Y	★ ★ ★ ★ ★	Greatly improved lung volume and function and proper breathing mechanics. I use this every day and plan to continue forever. Increased lung volume by > 50% in one week of use.
Grounding/ earthing (G google it)	Y	★ ★ ★ ★ ★	Reduced inflammation, promotes feeling of well being. I use Grounding mats while barefoot in my home while seated and I sleep in a grounding mat that goes under my sheets. The principle of earthing or grounding to the earth's magnetic and electrical field is based in solid science. The book Earthing gives the scientific background.
Mindful walking/ walking meditation (habit stacking)	Y	★ ★ ★ ★ ★	Promotes immediate calmness and lower heart rate.
Probiotics and prebiotics	Y	★ ★ ★ ★ ★	Important for intestinal health
Chia seeds I use organic white chia purchased on Amazon.	Y	★ ★ ★ ★ ★	Perfect balance of three omega oils 3,6,9. Also promotes bowel regularity. Chia seeds must be chewed and broken open, Otherwise they simply pass through your body and the omega oils are not released.
Left nostril breathing	Y	★ ★ ★ ★ ★	Promotes immediate calm and stress relief
Box breathing	Y	★ ★ ★ ★ ★	CardiovascularCardio vascular and mental health.

MCT oil I use High Octane Brain Oil from bulletproof.com	Y	★ ★ ★ ★ ★	Vast amount of empirical data on health benefits and immune support.
Tracking sleep metrics	Y	★ ★ ★ ★ ★	Morning andt bedtime 8 reps.
Tracking heart rate, SPO2, exercise minutes, calories daily.	Y	★ ★ ★ ★ ★	Invest in a smart watch. It pays great dividends in your health.
4-7-15 breathing	Y	★ ★ ★ ★ ★	Variation on 4-7-8 method that trains the diaphragm to completely exhale. PromotesPromots calmness.
Smart watch	Y	★ ★ ★ ★ ★	You can't manage what you can't measure. SmartphonesSmart phones provide tracking of health informationinformatio, reminders, and inspiration and challenge. MeditationMediation apps are highly valuable.
Neti pot	Y	★ ★ ★ ★ ★	Cleans stuffy nose, improves nasal breathing.
Beets or beet juice	Y	★ ★ ★ ★ ★	Well known for significant improvement in use of oxygen in exercise-- a secret weapon of athletes.
Daily Meditation practice	Y	★ ★ ★ ★ ★	Improves sense of well being, mood, sleep, attitude, productivity, calmness, composure, equanimity, joy, purpose. Decreases fear of the unknown and death.
Vitamin D	Y	★ ★ ★ ★ ★	Vital nutrient for immunity.

COLD Laser	Y	★ ★ ★ ★ ★	Reduced inflammation.n
Baking soda, one teaspoon 2x day to improve the alkalinity of the body.	Y	★ ★ ★ ★ ★	Helped prevent acidic body pH. Acidity promotes diseases and inflammation. inflamation
Delsym 12 hour extended release suspension.	Y	★ ★ ★ ★	Used for severalseverral months early in my IPF history. Helped persistent cough. Recommended by my pulmonologist as a "single ingredient" (dextromethorphan) cough suppressant that doesn't contain antihistamines or other side effect inducing ingredients.
Xarelto	Y	★ ★ ★ ★	Resolved pulmonary embolism in 45 days as verified by CT SCAN. Discontinued after resolution.
L Tryptophan	Y	★ ★ ★ ★	Improved sleep. Taken at bedtime.
Ned™ Sleep Blend	Y	★ ★ ★ ★	Good sleep aid with no side effects.
Vibration plate at 43MHz	Y	★ ★ ★ ★	Used Almost daily for 12 months. Effective for whole body exercise health. Google for research.
Salt room or salt inhalers	Y	★ ★ ★ ★	On the suggestion of my physician I used a Mockins Salt inhaler since there were no salt rooms in my area. Seems to help breathing, proper use of inhaler promotes diaphragmatic breathing. Have used it for 6 months.

Bulletproof Collagen	Y	★ ★ ★ ★	Improved joint flexibility and skin and nails.
Low level light therapy (laser)	Y	★ ★ ★ ★	I used this for lung inflammation and enlarged lymph nodes. NOTE: There were 30 papers on LLLT published in 2012 and there have been over 300 clinical trials and 3,000 laboratory studies on LLLT. There are also several ongoing studies at Harvard. The device is FDA approved, approved in Europe and Canada and used by high-level amateur and professional athletes worldwide. The four common clinical targets for LLLT are: Site of injury to promote healing, remodeling and reduce inflammation, Lymph nodes to reduce swelling and inflammation, Induction of analgesia or pain relief tTrigger points to reduce tenderness and relax contracted muscles
Prednisone	Y	★ ★ ★	Temporary relief during exacerbation of breathing problems but w/ long term bad side effects.
N Acetyl Cysteine	Y	★ ★ ★	Available without a prescriptionprescritption. Have used for 12 months. It appears to help with my recovery, is cheap and has no side effects. Clinical trials underway.

Acupressure	Y	★ ★ ★	Stopped coughing attacks by placing fingertip pressure on specific areas. More detail in book.
Turmeric Curcumen	Y	★ ★ ★	Effective as an anti-inflammatory. Promotes endothelial health.
Antibiotics	Y	★ ★	Helped pneumonia but b Bad side effects on gut health, which lowers immunity.
Chinese Herbs from WEI Institute and local practitioner	Y	★ ★	Seemed to have early results in the first 30 days, with greater energy and stamina but nNot effective long term.
Tessalon Pearls	Y	★ ★	Somewhat effective for cough.
PEMF Treatments	Y	★ ★	Inflammation relief.
Infrared Sauna	Y	★ ★	Anti-inflammatory.
Hydroxyzine for anxiety	Y	★ ★	It helped, but mindfulness meditation helped more.
Aromatherapy oils, eucalyptus lavender,mulling,	N	★	Smelled nice, no effectaffect on breathing. May help sleep.
Tylenol	Y	★	Reduces inflammation but side effects and long term use is not advised.
Medical Marijuana for anxiety	N	★	Helped forget anxiety but as it wore off it created rebound effects of anxiety and depression.
Air Phisio breath trainer	Y	★	May be helpful for breaking up phlegm but didn't strengthen diaphragm. Discontinued use.
Albuterol	N		Not effective for IPF.

Acupuncture	N		Not effective.
Montelucast/ Singulaire	N		No noticeable effect.
Budesonide	N		Didn't seem to help.
Black Cumin Seed oil	N		?
Ivermectin	N		Used frequently for Long CovVid. Unsure if it had any effect.
Vitamin C Intravenous mega doses	N		No noticeable effect.
Intravenous Ozone	N		No effect.
Maraviroc	N		Off label long CovVid treatment. Expensive, not effective.

Richard Goldberg M.D.
Prostate & Body Imaging

Roman Rozin M.D.
Musculoskeletal Imaging &
Minimally Invasive Pain Therapy

Shamit Sarangi M.D. CAQ
Neuroradiology

Kristina Siddall M.D.
Breast & Body Imaging

PARTNERS
IMAGING CENTERS

1250 S. Tamiami Trail
Suite 103
Sarasota, FL 34239

PH 941.951.2100
FX: 941.951.2110

3T Wide Bore MRI 1.5T MRI 64 slice CT / CTA PET/CT
Nuclear Medicine X-Ray Ultrasound Mammography Dexa

Patient Name: **Lee Fogle**
Account#   **2271020**
Date of Birth: **01/18/1958**
Referring Dr: **Craig Harcup**
Service Date: **08/06/2021**
Accession #:   **2119904-1**

CT ANGIOGRAPHY (CTA) OF THE THORAX

HISTORY: Post Covid-19 infection in January 2021. Pre-existing pulmonary interstitial fibrosis. Ongoing oxygen therapy. Evaluate for pulmonary fibrosis, pulmonary thromboembolism.

TECHNIQUE: Thin 2 mm contiguous axial images of the thorax were obtained following IV bolus injection of nonionic contrast (80 mL Optiray 350) on a Siemens HiSpeed 64-channel multidetector CT scanner. Post acquisition multiplanar reformatted images were created.

CTAC DOSE: Based on a 32 cm diameter phantom, the estimated radiation dose (CTDIvol [mGy]) for each series in this exam is 13.80, 1.58, 9.45, and 6 67. The estimated cumulative dose (DLP [mGy*cm]) is 718.

Partners Imaging CT scanners provide automated radiation dose reduction techniques including adjusting mAs and kV based on patient's size.

In house I-STAT serum creatinine = 0.7 mg/dl, eGFR = 100 mL/min/1.73 m2. COMPARISON: CT scan of the chest dated 3/26/2021 from Partners Imaging Center.

FINDINGS: There is a threadlike filling defect representing a nonobstructing thromboembolism beginning within the distal left interlobar pulmonary artery extending into the proximal lower lobe artery over an approximately 2 cm length. Pulmonary arteries are otherwise patent and normal in caliber visualized through to their subsegmental branches. No other filling defects or attenuation to suggest acute pulmonary thromboemboli. Main PA measures

2.5 cm in diameter, right PA 2.3 cm, left PA 2.3 cm.

Heart and its individual chambers are normal in size without filling defects. Thoracic aorta is normal in caliber. Origins to the great vessels are patent and in their usual anatomic alignment. Multiple borderline to slightly enlarged mediastinal lymph nodes are unchanged, a common appearance in association with advanced pulmonary fibrosis. Esophagus is nondistended and unremarkable throughout its course.

There are diffuse groundglass and reticular opacities with peripheral and basilar honeycombing associated with traction bronchiectasis, lung distortion, and volume loss. Findings represent end-stage pulmonary interstitial fibrosis, slightly progressed since prior exam. No pleural or pericardial effusions, thickening, or calcified plaques. No bony thorax or chest wall lesions. Limited, visualized portions of the liver, spleen, pancreas, adrenal glands, and upper poles of the kidneys are unremarkable.

IMPRESSION:

1. Nonobstructing threadlike thromboembolism within the distal left interlobar and proximal lower lobe pulmonary artery. Pulmonary arteries through to their subsegmental branches are otherwise patent without other acute pulmonary thromboembolism.
2. Interval slight progression of diffuse end-stage pulmonary interstitial fibrosis.
3. Stable multiple borderline to slightly enlarged mediastinal lymph nodes, commonly seen with advanced pulmonary fibrosis.

Electronically signed by: Richard Goldberg, MD 8/6/2021 12:45 PM

Thank you for your referral. If you have any questions or would like to discuss the results of this exam, I can be reached at the phone number on the top of this letterhead. A copy of this report, along with any key images, are available from the Partners Imaging Physician web portal http://picreports. com High resolution images are also available for viewing via our PACS client (on request).

Patient Name:	**Lee Fogle**
Account#	**2271020**
Date of Birth:	**01/18/1958**
Referring Dr:	**Craig Harcup**
Service Date:	**08/06/2021**

acute pulmonary thromboembolism.

4. Interval slight progression of diffuse end-stage pulmonary interstitial fibrosis.

5. Stable multiple borderline to slightly enlarged mediastinal lymph nodes, commonly seen with advanced pulmonary fibrosis.

Electronically signed by: Richard Goldberg, MD 8/6/2021 12:45 PM

Thank you for your referral. If you have any questions or would like to discuss the results of this exam, I can be reached at the phone number on the top of this letterhead. A copy of this report, along with any key images, are available from the Partners Imaging Physician web portal http://picreports.com High resolution images are also available for viewing via our PACS client (on request).

LEE FOGLE

Richard M. Goldberg, M.D.
Prostate & Body Imaging

Roman Rozin, M.D.
Musculoskeletal Imaging &
Minimally Invasive Pain Therapy

Shamit Sarangi, M.D. CAQ
Neuroradiology

Nicholas A. Dickson, D.O.
Breast and Body Imaging

PARTNERS
IMAGING CENTERS

Wide Bore High-Resolution MRI   CT / CTA   Digital X-Ray
Tomo Mammography   Ultrasound   DEXA   Breast Biopsies

5101 4th Ave Circle East
Suite 100
Bradenton, FL 34208

PH 941.782.0414
FX: 941.782.0418

Patient Name:	**Lee Fogle**
Account#	**2271020**
Date of Birth:	**01/18/1958**
Referring Dr:	**Ashley Dunmire Aprn**
Service Date:	**04/15/2022**
Accession #:	**2211280-1**

CTA chest with contrast

HISTORY
Follow-up, history of Covid, interstitial lung disease, on Xeralto

TECHNIQUE:
CTA of the chest was performed during intravenous administration of 80 cc Optiray 350 nonionic contrast, with multiplanar reconstructions performed, using a high-speed multidetector helical 64 slice CT scanner. Post processing 3D images were created. This scanner provides radiation dose reduction techniques using automated exposure control and mA and/or kV adjustment according to patient size.

COMPARISON:
1/25/2022, 8/6/2021

FINDINGS:
There is faint residual filling defect in a left lower segmental pulmonary artery consistent with small residual pulmonary embolus, image 52. There is no new filling defect or evidence of embolus. Main pulmonary arteries and central branches are patent and well-opacified. The aorta is normal in caliber. There is no pericardial effusion. There are coronary artery calcifications.

There is extensive stable honeycombing, lower zone predominant. There are groundglass opacities and extensive reticular interstitial opacities with architectural distortion and traction bronchiectasis. There is no confluent airspace disease. There is stable mediastinal and small right hilar adenopathy. There is no pleural effusion.

There is no supraclavicular or axillary adenopathy. The thyroid is normal in CT appearance. Limited images of the upper abdomen are unremarkable. The chest wall is normal in appearance.

IMPRESSION

1. Faint residual pulmonary embolus left lower segmental pulmonary artery. No new embolus.
2. Stable advanced pulmonary fibrosis.
3. Stable mediastinal and right hilar adenopathy.

Electronically signed by: Laura Kunberger, MD 4/15/2022 11:53 AM

Thank you for your referral. If you have any questions or would like to discuss the results of this exam, I can

Patient Name:	**Lee Fogle**
Account#	**2271020**
Date of Birth:	**01/18/1958**
Referring Dr:	**Ashley Dunmire Aprn**
Service Date:	**04/15/2022**

be reached at the phone number on the top of this letterhead. A copy of this report, along with any key images, are available from the Partners Imaging Physician web portal https://picreports.com   High resolution images are also available for viewing via our PACS client (on request).

LUNG ASSOCIATES OF SARASOTA
Associates in Sleep Medicine

BOARD CERTIFICATION
PULMONARY MEDICINE
CRITICAL CARE MEDICINE
INTERNAL MEDICINE * SLEEP MEDICINE

Bruce M. Fleegler, M.D., FCCP	Rabih H. Loutfi, M.D., FCCP*	Jennifer Caballero, PA-C
Craig H. Harcup, M.D., FCCP	Joseph C. Seaman, M.D., FCCP	Jeffrey Kienzle, P.A. - C
Kenneth M. Hurwitz, M.D., FCCP	Heidi R. Goedicke, M.D.	Tish A. Haight, A.P.R.N
Kisha J. Morgan, M.D., FCCP	Lakshmi Gowkanapalli Reddy, M.D.*	Emily C. Sylvain, A.P.R.N
Adel Asaad, M.D	Randall S. Schwartz, M.D.	Kayla A. Clemons, A.P.R.N
Amit Shah, M.D	Ziad W. Ghamra M.D	Beatriz Rose A.P.R.N.
Charles Pue M.D., FCCP		Amy Gasper A.P.R.N

Patient Name:	Lee Fogle	**ID#:**	432560
Date:	03/16/2021 10:42 AM	**Date of Birth:**	01/18/1958

History of Present Illness

The patient is a 63 year old male who presents to the practice today for a transition into care. The patient is transitioning into care from another physician and a summary of care was reviewed. the patient is a 63 year old white divorced male nonsmoker other than previous use of medical marijuana, who is seen now for increased shortness of breath.

Patient reports that he was well until January of 2020 when he had an episode of pneumonia associated with hypoxia, eventually treated with short course steroids antibiotic and bronchodilator. At that time there was concern he had Covid pneumonia, though apparently not tested, also having anosmia. He eventually improved, though in July of this year we presented with an apparent pneumonia Tampa General Hospital, at that time again treated with prednisone antibiotic and bronchodilators. Patient notes that he had some exposure to mold contamination prior to all this. Now he continue staff slowly progressive shortness of breath with exertion, although he is able to walk his dogs up to 10 blocks. in January and February of this year he had significant weight loss, and some fatigability though his weight has stabilized.

He has no recent fever chills or sweats headaches but has had coughing spasm nonproductive unassociated with hemoptysis. Occasional wheeze noted with chest tightness and occasional pleuritic-type at this discomfort. No recent nausea vomiting or diarrhea. He denies prior history of treated asthma emphysema prior history of pneumonia or tuberculosis. No history DVT or phlebitis. He does have history of narcolepsy had sleep studies years ago and previously treated, as well as some issue of anxiety related problems. He does not recall prior CAT scan, but apparently had been seen by pulmonologists and him of which escapes him.

Prio to his illness last year, he was a triatholon athlete.

Clinical Notes

05/21/2021 – Telemedicine

Consults - Outpatient

PULMONARY OUTPATIENT CONSULT NOTE

REFERRING PROVIDER
Dr. Harcup

REASON FOR CONSULT
Hypoxic respiratory failure

HISTORY OF PRESENT ILLNESS

Virtual visit performed via zoom.

Lee Fogle is a 63 y.o. male with a PMH of narcolepsy here for pulmonary consultation for hypoxic respiratory failure. Prior to Januar patient was a triathlete. In January 2020 he traveled by train to South Carolina to see his physician for narcolepsy and after noticed illness that he believes was COVID. Testing was not available at that time so he was never tested. He notes that his son drank out of his and seemed to exhibit similar symptoms for a few days. In May/ June 2020 he developed SOB that was becoming more pronounce cough. He was diagnosed with double pneumonia and oxygen saturation in the low 80s. He was treated with two rounds of prednise antibiotics and albuterol. He was offered oxygen during this but declined. In January 2021 he was seen by a pulmonologist who obta scan of the chest (no priors in his life), and an echocardiogram (images not available for review) and he was told he needs an open and patient came to Mayo clinic for a second opinion.

He endorses clubbing of the hands, dry cough, seborrheic dermatitis. He denies joint pains in the early morning, raynauds or other does endorse periods where he will have a high sugar food and will develop diffuse rashes and full body pain/aches.

He is currently prescribed NC oxygen at 3L/m at rest and 5 L/m with exercise. He does describe how he will take off his oxygen and an effort to build stamina. We discussed how this can be detrimental to his health and advised against this in the future.

SOCIAL HISTORY
-Worked as a software executive, denies any occupational chemical exposures
-Former smoker of marijuana, used a vape pen with marijuana for about 1 year
-No birds in the home but does have a down sofa for about 3 years
-Notes his sofa was in his old home where a pipe burst and caused molding and he believes the sofa likely has mold in it from this put a cover over it now
-Father worked as a cutter of asbestos when the patient was about 10 years old

Family history of father who died of emphysema and an asthma attack and was not a smoker

No Known Allergies

Active Home Medications

Medication	Sig	Taking
ASCORBIC ACID, VITAMIN C, IV	Infuse into a venous catheter as directed.	Yes
DME Oxygen	daily. DME Order	Yes
UNABLE TO FIND	as directed. "Platlet-Rich Plasma".	Yes
albuterol 5 mg/mL nebulizer solution	Inhale.	
albuterol 90 mcg/actuation inhaler	Inhale.	

History reviewed. No pertinent surgical history.

MEDICAL HISTORY REVIEW

Acknowledgments

The following people and organizations were instrumental in both helping me to overcome the lung disease that almost brought me to an early death and in inspiring me to write about my journey.

- o Noah Greenspan and his Ultimate Pulmonary Wellness organization, books and Bootcamp.
- o Ashley Dunmire, RN and Nurse Practitioner for her partnership in my health recovery
- o Jeff Sanow, retired CIA agent and friend who drove 70 miles one way twice a week to help me walk often for just a single block.
- o Dina Stewart, for her physical therapy, healing touch and her encouragement to write my story,
- o The Pulmonary Fibrosis Foundation, for their great work in education, awareness and support groups
- o Bruce Anderson, a fellow IPF patient who has used his own battle with IPF to help thousands of others through his support groups and website, PulmonaryCircles.com,
- o Dr. Michael Greger for his book <u>How Not to Die</u> and his non profit NutritionFacts.org education and research
- o The encouraging folks in my Pulmonary Circles Zoom support group led by Polly.

o   Leslie and Veronica who walked my dogs and encouraged me during my lowest point and ultimately gave me the inspiration to stop dying and start living!

Self-Publishing School

NOW IT'S YOUR TURN

Discover the EXACT 3-step blueprint you need to become a bestselling author in as little as 3 months.

Self-Publishing School helped me, and now
I want them to help you with this FREE
resource to begin outlining your book!

Even if you're busy, bad at writing, or don't know where to
start, you CAN write a bestseller and build your best life.

With tools and experience across a variety of niches
and professions, Self-Publishing School is the <u>only</u>
resource you need to take your book to the finish line!

DON'T WAIT

Say "YES" to becoming a bestseller:

https://self-publishingschool.com/friend/

Follow the steps on the page to get a FREE resource
to get started on your book and unlock a discount
to get started with Self-Publishing School

About the Author

Lee Fogle is a retired global technology entrepreneur and CEO with three adult children and two grandchildren. Since the age of 50 he has been an avid triathlete and Ironman™ triathlete. In his spare time he has led numerous humanitarian missions to India, Jamaica and Africa where he and his son helped to finance and build the Neema Children's Home in Kisumu, Kenya for AIDS orphans. He has taught life skill courses to current and former prison inmates in the US and Africa.

After contracting CoVid in January, 2020, Lee's health declined dramatically, resulting in pneumonia and end-stage pulmonary fibrosis. Through personal research, trial and error, exercise, breath training, nutrition, meditation and fasting he aggressively battled the near fatal disease and has recovered his health and vitality. He serves on multiple lung disease support groups where he teaches the methods used in his own recovery.

Lee is currently a hospice volunteer and a Death Doula in training and teaches elderly groups the principles for healthy aging. He lives on the gulf coast of South Florida where he enjoys cycling, golfing, swimming, reading, writing, learning and long walks in nature with his two dogs, Lucy and Nemo.

Can You Help?

Thank You For Reading My Book!

I really appreciate all of your feedback, and
I love hearing what you have to say.

I need your input to make the next version of
this book and my future books better.

Please leave me an honest review on Amazon letting
me know what you thought of the book.

Thanks so much!

Lee Fogle

Made in the USA
Las Vegas, NV
01 May 2024

89403649R00144